We Were
Baptized Too

We Were
Baptized Too

Claiming God's Grace for Lesbians and Gays

Marilyn Bennett Alexander
and
James Preston

Westminster John Knox Press
Louisville, Kentucky

Scripture quotations from the New Revised Standard Version of the Bible are copyright © 1989 by the Division of Christian Education of the National Council of Churches of Christ in the U.S.A. and are used by permission.

Copyright © 1992 by Houghton Mifflin Company. Reprinted by permission from THE AMERICAN HERITAGE DICTIONARY OF THE ENGLISH LANGUAGE, THIRD EDITION.

Book design by Jennifer K. Cox
Cover design by Alec Bartsch
The stained-glass artwork on the cover is from the Community Window of the Cathedral of Hope, Metropolitan Community Church, Dallas, Texas, and is used by permission.

First edition

Published by Westminster John Knox Press
Louisville, Kentucky

This book is printed on acid-free paper that meets the American National Standards Institute Z39.48 standard. ♾

PRINTED IN THE UNITED STATES OF AMERICA

96 97 98 99 00 01 02 03 04 05 — 10 9 8 7 6 5 4 3 2

Library of Congress Cataloging-in-Publication Data

Alexander, Marilyn Bennett, 1961–
   We were baptized too : claiming God's grace for lesbians and gays / Marilyn Bennett Alexander and James Preston. — 1st ed.
      p.   cm.
   Includes bibliographical references.
   ISBN 0-664-25628-7 (alk. paper)
   1. Gays—Religious life.   2. Lesbians—Religious life.   3. Homosexuality—Religious aspects—Christianity.   I. Preston, James, 1964–   .   II. Title.
BV4596.G38A42   1996
261.8'35766—dc20   95-46241

For my niece, Madeleine Elizabeth.
May she never doubt that she is a child of God.

◆

For my life partner, LM, and the gift of our loving

◆ Contents

◆ Foreword

What a poignant testimony this book turns out to be. It is a *cri de coeur* from the hearts of persons we have first accepted as baptized fellow Christians, members together with us all in the body of this Jesus Christ, wherein as a result of that baptism there is neither Jew nor Greek, male nor female, free nor slave—there is a radical equality.

And then we spurn them, we shun them, because we are all caught up in an acknowledged or a tacit homophobia and heterosexism. We reject them, treat them as pariahs, and push them outside the confines of our church communities, and thereby we negate the consequences of their baptism and ours.

We make them doubt that they are the children of God, and this must be nearly the ultimate blasphemy. We blame them for something that it is becoming increasingly clear they can do little about. Someone has said that if this particular sexual orientation were indeed a matter of personal choice, then gay and lesbian persons must be the craziest coots around to choose a way of life that exposes them to so much hostility, discrimination, loss, and suffering. To say this is akin to saying that a black person voluntarily chooses a complexion and race that exposes him- or herself to all the hatred, suffering, and disadvantages to be found in a racist society. Such a person would be stark raving mad.

This book contains a searing indictment of our quite uncomfortable position regarding homosexuality. It is only of homosexual persons that we require universal celibacy, whereas for others we teach that celibacy is a special vocation. We say that sexual orientation is morally a matter of indifference, but what is culpable are homosexual acts. But then we claim that sexuality is a divine gift, which used properly, helps us to become more fully human and akin really to God, as it is this part of our humanity that makes us more gentle and caring, more self-giving and concerned for others than we would be without that gift. Why should we want all homosexual persons not to give expression to their sexuality in loving acts? Why don't we use the same criteria to judge same-sex relationships that we use to judge whether heterosexual relationships are wholesome or not?

I was left deeply disturbed by these inconsistencies and knew that the Lord of the Church would not be where his church is in this matter. Can we act quickly to let the gospel imperatives prevail as we remember our baptism and theirs, and be thankful?

DESMOND M. TUTU
ARCHBISHOP OF CAPE TOWN

◆ Acknowledgments

We want to acknowledge that the birthing of this book has been a mixture of joy, terror, and ambivalence. Without a strong circle of friends and loved ones, we would not have given life to this book. First, we thank Birdie Barr, who provided us with laughter, scary movies, food, grounding, and a strong shoulder to lean on.

Thanks to the many people who gave insight to the book, especially our readers at various stages of creation: Marjorie Procter-Smith, Danna Nolan Fewell, Jo Carr, Mel White and Gary Nixon, Bobby McMillan, Daniel Humbert, Sondra Stalcup, Dixie Robertson, Elaine Copeland, Kim Reed, and Matt Wehrly.

We would not have been able to see the fruits of our labors without the gifts of time and computer expertise from Janice Virtue and Matt Wehrly. For research and documentation, we thank Tammy Sherwood and Lemar Rodgers. To all who submitted stories—bringing us inspiration and giving the book greater depth—we are grateful.

James gives special thanks to the congregations, staff, and supporters of the Reconciling Congregation Program for their vision and hope. Appreciation is also expressed for the love and support of the staff and Disciple Bible Study Group at St. John's United Methodist Church, the youth workers support group, and the lectionary study group—all in Lubbock, Texas.

Marilyn acknowledges the support of her colleagues and friends at Perkins School of Theology, the No Therapy Lunch Group, the women's book group at Cathedral of Hope Metropolitan Community Church, Respect All Youth (RALLY), and Lambda. Thanks to Karen Helfert for wisdom, guidance, and nurture. To the camping community of Flathead Lake United Methodist Senior High Camp, Mon-

tana, she offers thanks for golden moments of liberation and cru-
cibles of struggle and challenge. To my family, especially my coura-
geous mother, thanks for standing with me—don't worry, the television cameras are not running.

We give special thanks for the scheming ways of Mpho Tutu, who
was instrumental in giving our manuscript to her father. Deep and
heartfelt gratitude to Archbishop Desmond Tutu, who read the book
and gave us great words of encouragement during immense historical change in his own country of South Africa. We were touched by
his commitment to the liberation of all God's children.

Special thanks to our editor, Jon Berquist, for his commitment to
publishing this manuscript and guiding us through the editorial
maze. To all at Westminster John Knox Press, we are grateful.

And finally, we offer deep appreciation for each other and our abil-
ity to challenge, stretch, and love one another along this journey. We
have come a long way from that fear-ridden conversation in a church
parking lot eight years ago.

◆ Introduction

Both of us have traveled different paths that have intersected at many points along the way. We share a common ministry within the United Methodist Church, though the forms have varied over the years. Many times, however, we found ourselves, in coffee shops, church parking lots, and spiritual life retreats, coming back to the same question: What does it mean to be Christian and gay? Having had lifelong commitments to the church, we knew the profound impact of the liberating Christ in our lives. We have been tempted to leave the church, but somewhere in our hearts was a stirring, a calling to remain. We believe the water of our baptisms is the source of that persistent call.

Every Sunday morning, mainline Christian congregations across this country welcome into their fold newly baptized Christians, children of God. Within the liturgy, these congregations pledge their undying support to accept, love, forgive, and nurture this person in the faith. Yet the church honors this covenant selectively. For what was supposed to be a means of unconditional love, grace, and justice becomes a conditional covenant for lesbian and gay Christians—a compromise ending in silence, oppression, and judgment. It is this church that obstructs God's grace and leads gay men and lesbians to doubt that they are children of God.

Lesbian women and gay men can no longer remain silent while the mainline church distorts God's sacramental grace and justice. No longer can mainline heterosexual Christians dis-member the silenced brothers and sisters in their midst. *We Were Baptized Too* challenges the church to take seriously its understanding of Baptism and Communion as a means of grace, justice, and liberation. This book exemplifies how the church leads gay/lesbian Christians from baptism to silence and labeling as "stranger"; from confidence as a child of God to isolation, alienation, and condemnation. Between the chapters are interludes in which eight gay/lesbian Christians tell their own stories of struggle and faith. The book shows a progression from doubt to celebrative reclaiming of one's identity as a child of God through a renewed understanding of Baptism/Communion and through stories of empowerment in the face of estrangement and silence. This act of reclaiming is an act of faith. The church re-members.

We Were Baptized Too is a hopeful call for a renewed vision of a truly inclusive church where all God's children—gay or non-gay—can live knowing whose child they are. We hope that this book will challenge, affirm, and transform you. We know from our own experience that the journey toward liberation and justice does not bypass pain or confusion. Therefore, appendix B provides a reflection sheet to help you process your thoughts and feelings along the way. At times you may want to abandon this book out of anger or fear. We encourage you to take time out for yourself, let your emotions rise and fall, and return to the book and the journey. Also, in living out our baptismal vision, we have created worship resources to assist churches and individuals in affirming themselves and the gay/lesbian persons in their midst (see Appendix A).

Gifts That We Bring

We come to this book acknowledging our gifts and our limitations. We bring the breadth of both the lesbian and gay experience, yet we admit that our Anglo, middle-class, able-bodied perspective restricts our knowledge of the broader experience of potential readers. The chapters will reflect our own diversity in the writing styles, coming-out stories, and gender politics. Often the word *gay* is used to represent the entire gay/lesbian community, but in reality, gay men as men are privileged over women in general in the areas of economics, job opportunities, salary equity, health care, and gender-role expectations. In comparison to women, gay men, as privileged males, do not face in the same way the daily threats of sexual harassment, lost reproductive rights, and violence. We do not intend to collapse the lesbian experience into the gay experience but to hold out each as liberating and equal gifts to the other. In accordance with this understanding, chapters 2 through 5 each have a distinctive style, reflective of our individual experience and coming-out process during the writing of this book. James primarily authored chapters 2 and 4; Marilyn, 3 and 5. The epilogue reflects where we are now as we prepare to publish this manuscript three years after its inception. The stories you will read offer a snapshot of a particular time in our lives; the epilogue, yet another. The gifts we offer are only partially representative of the rich and beautiful fabric of the lesbian, gay, bisexual, and transgender community. Therefore, we have at least included stories of other gays and lesbians to show the diversity, end the silence and estrangement, and witness to God's continual love and acceptance.

Naming Ourselves

We assert the right to name ourselves and define our own experience. Throughout the book we will use the term *gay/lesbian* rather than "gay men and lesbians" or *homosexual*. "Gay/Lesbian" symbolizes the unity in the midst of diversity. "Gay/Lesbian refers to the sexual difference between gay men and lesbian women and their common experience of homophobic oppression."[1] The term "homosexual" restricts the focus to sexual acts. Later in the book we will also use the term *Queer* as an inclusive term for the lesbian and gay community and as a means of political and social commitment. In the words of gay activist Robert Goss, "*Queer* is a term of political dissidence and sexual difference. It is part of the movement to reclaim derogatory words from oppressive culture."[2] We cannot claim to represent the bisexual and transgender experience in the scope of this book, though that concern is present.

We claim our Christian identity with great humility and deep commitment. Primarily, the *Christian Church* has oppressed, marginalized, and rejected gays/lesbians throughout its history. It is difficult to claim to be a part of such a Church. Yet we believe in the commitment of Jesus Christ to liberate and empower all people. It is this belief that we bring to this book.

Naming Our Theology

Our theology reflects our longtime commitment to the United Methodist Church and naturally is not representative of all mainline denominations. Our theology is greatly guided by John Wesley's understanding that the Christian faith can be interpreted through the lens of the quadrilateral, that is, through the interplay of scripture, reason, tradition, and experience.[3] We believe that the experience of lesbian and gay Christians has been neglected, many times rejected, and therefore excluded from church traditions. Scripture has been used as a weapon against gay/lesbian Christians. Similarly with the use of reason, we also want to point out that though numerous psychological, sociological, and biological studies have found homosexuality and bisexuality to be healthy and normal sexual orientations, the church primarily refuses to accept these studies as compelling reasons to embrace the lives of lesbians and gays as valid witnesses to the Christian faith. We want to again acknowledge the vital importance of all components of the quadrilateral.

Three concepts need clarification at this point. When we refer to the Church with a capital C, we are speaking of the Body of Christ in a universal sense. When we use the term church with a lowercase c, we are writing about a local congregation, a denomination, or any structure or institutional agency connected with a denomination. When using the phrase "child of God" or "children of God," we are directly referring to baptized Christians or candidates for baptism. We do not want to imply that those outside the Christian faith are outside God's care, love, or acceptance; neither are they due any less respect or dignity. We also admit the limits of the image of "child of God" to reflect fully our relationship with God as mature adults living out our baptismal call.

Scripture

Too often the valid witness of faith of gay/lesbian Christians has been rejected due to a misconstrued or distorted interpretation of scripture. Not only are skewed views of scripture used by homophobic pastors and church leaders, but many times reporters and politicians instantly become biblical quoters when the issue of homosexuality surfaces. God forbid that these same persons would utilize scripture when facing the issues of economics and social welfare. As New Testament scholar Victor Paul Furnish reminds us, "I find this quite remarkable, considering that the writings we refer to as 'the Bible' have no civil or public authority in the United States. They are regarded as scriptural only within specific religious communities. . . . And yet, in quite public and secular forums, the Bible is regularly invoked on this specific topic of homosexuality."[4] Unfortunately, the Bible is often used within and without the church as a selective weapon of oppression rather than as a tool for liberation.

In this instance, scripture has been so overused and understudied that we regret the need to enter into this dialogue about scripture and homosexuality. Yet we realize as Christians that any serious discussion of faith must involve the study of scripture. We will, therefore, briefly address the following passages because they have been used as swords of oppression instead of plowshares of love. For we, like the prophet Micah, dream of a day when we shall all sit under our own vines and our own fig trees and no one shall make the other afraid (Mic. 4:3–4).

The word *homosexual* was not even in use in the English language until 1897, and it first appeared in a biblical translation in 1952 with the release of the Revised Standard Version. The original biblical languages of Hebrew and Greek have no word for homosexuality, let alone specific vocabulary to connote any particular understanding of sexuality, gender identity, or sexual orientation.[5]

Genesis 19 and Judges 19 are stories of gang rape and protection of male visitors.[6] They address violence toward and subjugation of men. They are not about men loving men; they are about men forcing other men into humiliated submission (the same low status of women).[7] As Lindsey Louise Biddle notes, "The story of Sodom frequently gets used to promote homophobia and gay-bashing; it almost never serves to condemn rape or misogyny or xenophobia. Using this tale about hospitality to preach hatred and to justify exclusion of others is like using Jesus' parable of the Good Samaritan as a basis for anti-Semitism or priest bashing—it misses the whole point of the story."[8] And to quote another scholar, Peter Gomes, "To suggest that Sodom and Gomorrah is about homosexual sex is an analysis of about as much worth as suggesting that the story of Jonah and the whale is a treatise on fishing."[9]

Leviticus 18:22 and 20:13 are verses that focus on men and their role within a patriarchal society. They have nothing to do with gay/lesbian love; in fact, lesbian sex is not even prohibited. In their book *Gender, Power, and Promise*, Danna Nolan Fewell and David M. Gunn write, "For readers bent on culling from the Bible a blanket condemnation of 'homosexuality' this omission [lesbian sex] is an embarrassment. It is, however, eminently understandable. The text does not construct an essential category of 'homosexuality' but rather it defines sexual boundaries which are part of the construction of patriarchy through the privileging of male control of seed."[10] This segment of the Holiness Code in Leviticus was part of an overall effort to maintain the identity of a minority culture and religion.[11]

First Corinthians 6:9–11 and 1 Timothy 1:10 do not address homosexuality, but focus on idolatrous activity.[12] The problem with both passages is the ambiguity of the translations of two important words: *arsenokoites* (NRSV: *sodomites*) and *malakos* (NRSV: *male prostitutes*).[13] The writers of these passages were concerned with the matter of male prostitution and pederasty (adult men having sex with boys), not with mutual, loving relationships between two adult men.[14]

Romans 1:26–27 is certainly the most specific text about same-gender sex. It is also the only scriptural passage that mentions sex between women. Yet it must be noted that Paul had no understanding of modern sexual identity, of sexual orientation, or of the possibility of same-gender covenantal love relationships.[15] Paul is not specifically singling out homosexual acts, but he borrows a standard Hellenistic list of moral failings.[16] Homoerotic acts were considered evil in a Hellenistic culture because they were thought to be motivated by lust, did not promote procreation, and abandoned the traditional gender roles of a patriarchal society.[17]

Our effort here has been to give you a basic look at the Bible and its mention of homosexuality. Recently, we saw a brochure whose cover brazenly stated *What Jesus Said About Homosexuality!* On opening it, we found nothing but blank white space. Again we were reminded that homosexuality is barely mentioned in the scriptures. If this had been a brochure adamantly stating *What Jesus Said About Loving Your Neighbor,* we would have found verse after verse about God's covenant, community, and grace. The Bible is not preoccupied with homosexuality, but with justice, kindness, and humility.[18]

Oppression Is the Issue

Many times the quest for gay/lesbian justice gets sidetracked by arguments over the choice to be gay/lesbian versus being born gay/lesbian. Often the discussion centers on whether homosexuality is compatible with Christian teaching. The mission of the church becomes a duel over who is in and who is out, who is deserving and who is not.

Gays/Lesbians frequently are accused of promoting a mythological "gay agenda." In recent years, this misconception has distorted the fight for basic civil rights and has led to such atrocities as anti-gay referendums, ordinances, and amendments that deny basic civil rights to people based on the reality of who and how they love. Gays/Lesbians are not asking for special rights but rather the basic rights afforded all persons: protection from physical violence, non-discrimination in housing, job security, and the same fundamental legal options that heterosexual couples enjoy. When heterosexual couples are entitled to dual insurance benefits, joint tax returns, and church/state-blessed covenantal marriages, we certainly do not label these as "special rights." Likewise, why should we be afraid to honor gay/lesbian relationships by granting these unions the same basic rights?[19] The Church does not need to be sidetracked by the argument of privileges versus rights, but it can continue its mission to fight for justice and salvation for all people.

We want to be very clear: Oppression is the issue. We start at a place of God's baptismal mark on us—God's love and acceptance—and we move forward stirred by God's desire for everyone to be free from fear, free from hatred, free from hopelessness. Let not the Church be distracted by homophobic and heterosexist baggage. Let the Church be infused with liberation.

1 ◆ We Remember Our Baptism

Marilyn

On a crisp Dakota Sunday morning, tightly wrapped against the November cold, I was carried off to the town's Methodist church to be the delight of the baptizing family of God. Cheery smiles and wiggling fingers greeted my arrival on this important day. The hymns in the morning light sounded for me the story of God's love, of the Savior's compassion. I was in the House of Unconditional Love, the Church, bundled in joy and expectation.

The pastor's strong arms kept me safe even as his wet, dripping hand touched my silky curled head, and his booming voice spoke God's blessing. The chorus of congregants rang out their earnest commitment to love and guide this little one, and God smiled that they had once again remembered the love that has no end.

My brothers and sister stood proudly showing off their baby sister; my parents smiled at each other and their many loved ones around them: another child promised to God, another reminder of God's grace for all.

Thirty-two years later, I remember my baptism. The church does not.

I remember my baptism. The church does not. Why else would it deny me my identity? Why else would it so adamantly preach "Don't ask, don't tell"? To the church, lesbians are not Christians first and foremost, but decadent, unfaithful perverts set out to destroy the very fabric of society. So how could a lesbian have been baptized?

How does anyone come to be baptized? How can anyone claim to be worthy of the touch of God? Is it not God who claims worth, and

1

does not God claim each infant, child, and adult as sacred and worthy of supreme love?

I believe this. I believe to my very core that God loves me and that this love is as precious as fine jewels. This love is the love to be emulated in all our relationships. This love is to be a means of grace, a balm to our souls, an inspiration to our hearts, and a rock on which to stand. I do believe that Jesus loves the little children, *all* the children of the world. I do believe that God will never forsake me, never leave me.

And this is why I have such hope for the Church, the body of Christ, which is to exemplify this love: the body that is to further this love at all costs. Weaving through the daily-ness of its essential life are the sacraments: Baptism and Communion. One is the initial act of God; the other, a constant reminder.

Where does the Church go wrong? Is it in baptizing lesbian infants, or in not fulfilling the covenant made at an infant's baptism? Is it in asking the child grown up to give of her prayers, presence, gifts, and service, but not of her true identity, her authentic being in the world? Is it, in fact, in asking her to be a silent conspirator to her own demise, her own un-health; teaching her self-hatred rather than self-love, teaching her neglect of self, teaching her to mask her identity with "faithful" platitudes from societal standards instead of from a loving heart?

In Baptism, words of faith are spoken, petitions of prayer are offered, and support of loved ones is affirmed. These were the words spoken at my baptism:

> Dearly beloved, forasmuch as all men are heirs of life eternal and subjects of the saving grace of the Holy Spirit; and that our Saviour Christ saith, "Suffer the little children to come unto me, and forbid them not, for of such is the kingdom of God"; I beseech you to call upon God the Father, through our Lord Jesus Christ, that of his bounteous goodness he will grant unto Marilyn Adele Bennett, now to be baptized, the continual replenishing of his grace that she become a worthy member of Christ's holy Church.
> *Then the congregation prayed:*
> Almighty and everliving God, we beseech thee that of thine infinite goodness thou wilt look upon Marilyn Adele Bennett and grant that by the aid of thy Holy Spirit she may be steadfast in faith, joyful through hope, and rooted in love, and that she may so live the life which now is, that she may

enter triumphantly the life which is to come; through Jesus Christ our Lord. Amen.

Then the minister addressed the parents:

Dearly beloved, forasmuch as Marilyn Adele Bennett is now presented by you for Christian baptism, and is thus consecrated to God and to his Church, it is your part and duty to see that she be taught, as soon as she shall be able to learn, the meaning and purpose of this holy Sacrament; that she be instructed in the principles of our holy faith and the nature of the Christian life; that she shall be trained to give reverent attendance upon the public and private worship of God and the teaching of the Holy Scripture; and that in every way, by precept and example, you shall seek to lead her into the love of God and the service of our Lord Jesus Christ.

Do you solemnly promise to fulfill these duties so far as in you lies, the Lord being your helper?

The parents responded: We do.[1]

"Steadfast in faith." I *have* been steadfast in the faith in that I have had to trust God and only God with my true self, for I cannot trust the church, my family, colleagues, the judicial system governing me, the military, my city council, the police force, my neighborhood watch group, my boss, or my sisters and brothers in the faith. I cannot trust the grace of my childhood. I can only trust God. So, yes, I have been established in the faith. I have also become cynical and skeptical in the faith, as well as distrustful, paranoid, intimidated, torn, fearful, and silent.

The silence is deafening. The silence is so loud that sometimes I cannot even hear the voice of God nor the proclamation of grace for me. The silence roars over the words offered as I receive the body and blood of Christ. The silence begs me, with church-sanctioned fear, to stay quiet, to remain hidden to avoid inviting shame.

In the implosive silence, my story of faith rages within my soul, and my spirit shrivels without the infusion of life, without the breath, *ruach*,[2] to give my story form. Oh, the utter sadness of God's grace not shared, the utter despair of self-neglect.

Now, the time has come, however, to tell my story, breaking the tyranny of silence to stand against shameful injustice. It is time to proclaim God's goodness over the Church's inhospitality. Let the prisoners shout, "Freedom. Freedom is coming. Yes, this I know."[3]

Freedom comes for those who fight for justice, for those who withstand being labeled "militant," "radical," or "privilege-seeking."

Freedom comes by staking a claim for one's reality in a world of "majority rule". It comes with those who risk the life they know for the life they dream can be. For this woman-loving woman, the dream is to openly live out my faith in a God whose creative desire is for us to be a blessing to each other, to value each one's sacred spirit, and to fight against the evils of hatred, greed, and alienation. The dream is to stand strong in the face of rejection and ridicule with the knowledge that the unconditional love of God is more powerful than the hatred of a society afraid.

I can see the thread of love woven tightly into my life journey as a woman-loving woman. Throughout my faith development, God was there and so were gay and lesbian Christians. I tell my story as an affirmation of faith.

I was raised on United Methodist Sunday school literature, vacation Bible schools, red Kool-Aid in Dixie cups, and homemade Christmas ornaments. My faith was formed on choir retreats, mission trips, and youth programs. My faith was tested by campus ministry bus breakdowns and all-night hunger vigils. Cross talks, hunger walks, lock-ins, lock-outs, seminary study groups, and denominational conference presentations marked my years with meaning and challenge, creating a loving and seeking faith. But with all the richness of my church life, I still stand at a turning point, calling into question the church's rejection of its baptismal promise, the breaking of a vow that the family of God upheld as I grew to adulthood.

At other times, the church could have countered its earlier promise. Maybe it is a franchise problem. Can one congregation hold another responsible for its promises? For instance, by the time I entered the confirmation program we were members of a Methodist church in Oklahoma. Should this new group of people be held responsible for the first group's promise?

Evidently so. Again more words were spoken in support of me at the time that I confirmed my faith, when I took on for myself the faith that had been claimed on my behalf as an infant.

> Dearly beloved,
> the church is of God,
> and will be preserved to the end of time,
> for the conduct of worship
>   and the due administration of his Word and Sacraments,
> the maintenance of Christian fellowship and discipline,
> the edification of believers,
> and the conversion of the world.

All, of every age and station,
    stand in need of the means of grace which it alone supplies.

After my renunciation of sin and profession of faith, my pastor
laid his hands on my head and said:

Marilyn Adele Bennett, the Lord defend you with his
    heavenly grace
and by his Spirit confirm you
    in the faith and fellowship
    of all true disciples of Jesus Christ.

The people responded: *Amen*.

And my pastor spoke again:

Brethren,
I commend to your love and care
    Marilyn whom we this day receive
    into membership of this congregation.
Do all in your power
    to increase her faith,
    confirm her hope,
    and perfect her in love.[4]

I want to stop here a moment as if we were looking at a snapshot
because, really, it was a significant occasion. Here is my pastor, blessing me at the time of my confirmation. What is significant is that my
pastor, a publicly self-avowed heterosexual married man, was known
to have had a hidden gay life. This retired bishop later died of AIDS,
presumably contracting this virus through his gay sexual affairs.[5]
    It was because of him that as a fifth grader, I first heard the word
"homosexual." But others described the same man as "authoritarian,
aggressive, manipulative and deceitful."[6] I listened to adults in the
church angrily discussing this man's abuses of pastoral authority and
the infidelity in his marriage through sexual affairs with men.[7] To
many, the words "abusive" and "homosexual" have not been disen-
tangled, and the word "homosexual" has come to be the all-encompassing representation of all that is negative.
    I refer to that snapshot because of a reference I heard at General
Conference, the National United Methodist meeting in Louisville,
Kentucky, in 1992. I was talking to a brilliant, usually thoughtful pastor during a break between sessions. He was telling me that gays just
needed to be patient. Pastors just needed time to observe these so-
called monogamous and committed long-term gay relationships to

see if they were truly good relationships in order for the church to decide whether or not homosexuality should be branded "incompatible with Christian teaching." He went on to say that the church already had one example of a gay life, a gay bishop for that matter.

I cringed at several points. First, why would we assume that it is appropriate for heterosexuals to make decisions about the meaning of homosexuality? Second, what would the Church see from observing a heterosexual marriage? Statistics on child and wife abuse? Or role models for equality and mutuality? I bet not. Would the same question be asked, "Is heterosexuality compatible with Christian teaching?" Not likely. And finally, to me, a man who clearly hid his sexual orientation, and who sometimes abused his pastoral authority—though in later years showed much compassion and concern for the gay community—is not the best role model as a bishop, let alone a gay man in this day and time.[8]

At the time of the conference, in order not to out myself and thus jeopardize my job, I could only answer, "Every second that the church takes to make up its mind, gay and lesbian church members and nonmembers, their parents, lovers, children, and siblings will be in pain. How long will the church take?"

I felt sorry for the man. He actually thought he had part of the solution. He told me that because pastors are often privy to information that parishioners are not, that he knew of several gay couples in his church. Knowing this, if he were just allowed to watch them for a time, he would be able to make his decision about gays and lesbians. In his short-sightedness, it had not occurred to him that he might be talking to a real live *lesbian,* who was deeply insulted by his presumptions about what he knew because of his office as pastor.

The saddest part of all was that he is one of the better ones—ones who should understand—no, ones who should take the initiative simply to listen to and value the insight of those who do understand.

I suppose that to *understand* was his intent: he would observe and then he would understand. However, homosexuality, like gender, race, culture, or age group, cannot be understood by simply observing; persons outside the experience can never be fully aware of it. To me, it is more honest and respectful to admit to being an outsider incapable of full understanding, though capable of compassion, imagination and friendship.

I remember my reaffirmation of my baptism at age seventeen in the church chapel of yet another United Methodist Church, this one in Texas (the oil industry in which my father worked kept moving companies in business). I remember the pastor who laid his hands on my head and the three friends present. I thought then that I understood baptism, the Holy Spirit's work in my life, and being "born again." I had a new awakening of God's life inside me. I felt I was a new person.

I did not know that pastor would, thirteen years later, be pushed out of a pastoral appointment for taking a stand in favor of gays and lesbians. I did not know that one of my three friends was also lesbian. I did not know, but God did.

I went on to marry a man and to try and live out the prescribed life. I entered a heavy depression that took years to break; I felt trapped in a prison with no way to communicate to those outside, no way to call for help. In many ways, I did not know why I was so unhappy.

Through the friendship of yet another woman-loving woman, rays of sunlight—though heavily clouded—tried to break into my cell; but, the love I felt for her terrified me even more. I thought my whole life was coming apart. The fear was unbearable; but, I felt that there was no one to whom I could entrust my emerging self. I wrote cryptic notes in my prayer journal, disguising my feelings to an unlikely reader. I felt I had no one to whom I could turn; but, in the darkness, I did know that God heard my prayer and would not abandon me.

The gift of that time that I could enjoy was the wonderful theological discussions with my new friend. She pushed me to think and read and think some more. She challenged me to move beyond my obsession to "save" people to a desire to fight for social justice. She filled my mind with books such as *Cry of the People*, *The Color Purple*, and *Texts of Terror*.[9]

With the help of the United Methodist Church in which I was a member at the time, I began to enlarge my language of God and to see myself less as a sinner and more as one created in the image of God. It was only a beginning, but it set the stage for a new life.

I moved from that church home in Montana back to Texas to enter seminary. One of the first people I met was a lesbian who was to further my understanding of God's gift of sexuality. She also gave me books to read, such as *Is the Homosexual My Neighbor?*,[10] carefully wrapped in a paper sack so our classmates would not discover the contents.

In the course of two years, it seemed that homosexuality came up in conversations all the time. Once on a trip to the dentist, I was asked to stay after my appointment to talk to the dentist. He was struggling with the sexual identity of one of his beloved Sunday school students and wanted to know the United Methodist's stand on homosexuality. My anesthetized lips and mouth kept me from saying a whole lot, though I tried to mutter, "Itsth vaary com-pli-cathed."

I began to discern who were the gays in the entering seminary classes. My gay-sensor was of great use to my gay and lesbian friends. More and more college friends were "coming out" to me. In preaching classes, I began to preach the good news *for* gay men and lesbians; and in the process, a close friend and mentor pointed out to me that I created an "us" and "them" dichotomy. I glimpsed my own self-fear that lobbied for distance. This time, though, I was strong enough to admit to myself that I might be one of "them."

Depression competed against personal growth and threatened to keep me passive, but the diagnosis of my father's cancer jarred me, reminding me of life's finitude. I awakened to the realization that life was too short to live by someone else's plan. Through my separation and divorce, I did not know I would someday claim to be a lesbian, but I think God did. I have had too many wonderful friendships that have helped to guide and support me in my time of need to give up totally the idea of divine providence.

It would be three more years before I could bridge the distance of self-fear, and only then did I begin to own the pain, prejudice, and self-doubt. Only then did I see the Church's role as an accomplice to my self-hatred and self-rejection. Only then did I begin to rebuild my faith and trust in the supreme love of God and find the breadth and depth of human acceptance and love that was a balm to my soul, inspiration to my heart, and a rock on which to stand. The means of grace this time was the intimate love of a woman, my life partner.

You see, I am a lesbian. I am a woman-loving woman to whom the Church offers no place. The Church has room only for man-loving women. Call it sexist or homophobic, the Church will not hear you. There are a few United Methodist churches that open the doors— Reconciling Congregations to be sure. But others, even the ones that "*let* gays and lesbians in" do not have enough self-awareness to see that they have pushed Jesus away as the gatekeeper and replaced him with the whims of their own bias and prejudice.

Which brings me to a question: What is the Church to do about baptizing gay and lesbian babies?

That may sound absurd to you, maybe even unthinkable. It opens up old arguments about nurture versus nature and choice versus orientation; but, I ask the question seriously. How is the Church going to recognize babies into God's loving care with any integrity? As the child's sexuality emerges, will the Church squash the spirits of some into silence or, worse, lead the child to believe that he or she is banished from God's grace?

Perhaps the Church has been able to do this because by the time those gay and lesbian babies grow into adulthood, they have forgotten the words spoken at their baptism. But, I have not forgotten those words; and I believe that it is my covenantal responsibility to call the Church to remember them as well.

James

I have known about God and God's love for me for as long as I can remember. Some people recall the day they believed, and I surely can remember the day I joined the church or professed my faith. My Baptist family would say it was the day I was "saved." Yet, I really do not recall that my profession of faith was a major leap from somewhere else. It was more like another step in my journey of faith. It certainly was joyous and wonderful, but I would not say that the heavens opened up and angels sang. I have known for as long as I can remember about the love of God in Jesus Christ.

I have also known for as long as I can remember that something was different about me. I was able to figure out after several years that the difference (though I hate the word "difference") is that I love men. As a gay man, I want to be in a relationship with a man for life. "Coming out" as a gay man was certainly a bigger step then the one made regarding my initial profession of faith in my local Baptist church. It was like jumping from a sealed, darkened cave to a room where the light of dawn was breaking through the windows. I must say that "coming out" to myself (because I am still coming out) has been one of the most spiritual and faith-filled experiences of my life. It felt like what baptism into new life really should be.

My first memory of loving men occurred when I was five or six. My older cousin and I would pretend to be married, and I remember vividly dressing in my grandmother's apron and being his "wife." I have always recalled that particular set of memories throughout childhood and youth, and even now, sometimes I suddenly remember those thoughts and feelings in great detail. At that time, it did not seem like a great crime or even out of the ordinary. It seemed like a wonderful thing, and I would spend time with my imaginary friends talking about the day he and I would grow up and live together. But soon, my cousin and I were too old to play that game; and yet I began to understand that the game was not over for me. I kept thinking about guys.

As I entered adolescence, the innocence of my attraction to men became renamed as something strange. I do not mean to say that one day my mother and father said to me that my "pretend" fantasies were sick and should cease. They did not even know my thoughts and feelings. It was just indirectly conveyed that dreaming about guys was not the way boys acted—it was "sissy." Guys were only supposed to "pal around," not hug or kiss. I remember that during first and second grade the label of "sissy" did come my way at times, and it hurt. It hurt deeply. I remember being afraid of (and attracted to) the tougher guys in my elementary school. I thought about them frequently, but I do not think I could have understood that I was gay even then. There were no role models, tools or guides to naming, recognizing, or embracing my sexual identity. I realize now I was growing up as a homosexual kid, a Christian homosexual kid, and my Christian faith complicated my feelings even further.

I was nine years old when I decided it was time to be baptized. I had just been through membership training in my local Baptist church. I remember that Sunday morning very well. I was sitting by my parents during worship when the invitation was offered. The tears began to fall as the song was sung. My parents looked nervously at one another. I said to them, "I think I am ready to be baptized, to join the Church and to accept Jesus, Okay?" I suddenly stood up and made my way to the aisle. Walking up the aisle seemed like forever. The pastor smiled as he saw me walking toward him, and when I reached the front, he hugged and welcomed me. The last verse of "Just As I Am" had just been sung, and the tears began to slow down. Joy and happiness at my decision began to take their place. The pastor put his arm around me and announced that I was ready to profess faith in Jesus Christ and be baptized into the Church. He then asked for the congregation to vote for accepting me into their congregation—into the Church. The vote was taken, and I was elected unanimously into the congregation—everyone said "yes." That Christian body voted me into the Church, letting me into the faithful fold by pledging to nurture and support me as their brother. Now, that same church along with other churches that I have belonged to and served in, say "No! No! No! You are not worthy to be a child of God." These same Christians would vote me out of the Church, that is, reverse their decision concerning my faith. Unfortunately, they would make this decision based solely on their discovery of the missing pieces of my life—my homosexuality: the very thing that I consider a part of my continuing salvation.

I remember the faces of old women, the firm handshakes from hands that tilled the soil and planted the cotton, that surrounded me. I remember pats and hugs, words of welcome, tears of pride and joy and the words—"welcome——God bless you——we're so proud——welcome!" Where are those faces, hands, pats, and hugs now? They have been replaced by angry grimaces, closed fists, acts of violence, and the pain of rejection and silence. The covenant made that day lies somewhat intact due to the faithfulness of God, but part of it rests in a heap, shattered upon the tightly woven red carpet of a Baptist congregation, as well as upon the wooden chancel of a United Methodist congregation I now serve.

The night for my baptism had arrived. I wore blue jeans and a white T-shirt, common attire for the one being baptized. I met with the pastor in his office; there were others to be baptized as well. He prayed with us, and as he spoke I remember feeling such joy, acceptance, and love. We ascended the stairway and found ourselves looking into the pool of water, clear and tranquil. The pastor made his way into the water wearing his wading suit. The waters were no longer still, but they were troubled: churning, moving, rippling, sloshing. "Brother Bitner," as we called him, said words to those smiling faces and shaking hands of the Sunday morning before, and then I descended into the warm, almost nurturing water, with my handkerchief in hand. The water felt so comforting, like a womb, warm and suspended, poised to give birth to a new creation, a believer in Christ. That man held me tightly as he reassured me. He then plunged me deep within the warm, churning, and sloshing waters. In the midst of the gurgling bubbles, I heard the words, "Father, Son, and Holy Spirit" and I broke through the surface of the water. Something was now different as I heard the congregation say "Amen." I was marked, sealed, and washed as a child of God, a child of light and hope. It was this body, these fingers, this leg, and this heart which had been baptized. It was this smile, this hair, this soul, that had been washed in the womb of God. It was I, James, son, friend, chubby boy, laughing, sensitive, sometimes afraid, and most definitely gay who had been baptized. How can the church forget my baptism? How can those smiling faces, which would later watch me graduate, grow up, struggle, teach, preach, and be ordained, forget my baptism? I have not and God certainly has not, but many of them have.

My journey continued within the church as I struggled with "these feelings." I began to hate myself, and in response, I became more conservative and more fundamentalist in my faith. I lived a lie. As elementary life passed, junior high became a constant struggle of fear, inadequacy, and pain. I could never muster up the feelings to be attracted to the girls who surrounded me and decided to pursue a girl who dated other guys. It was almost as if I had chosen one I knew would say "no." The same story would repeat itself again in high school with another girl—someone who would never date me—and yet, I spent great amounts of energy trying to make it work. I tried to gain her attention, but I also knew it would never happen. Whenever the possibility was even remotely a reality, I would somehow say or do something to set her or her latest boyfriend into a mad fit. I finally gave up in my senior year, and another girl actually showed interest in me. We dated twice, but I felt nothing at all. The thought of kissing her just did not seem real. While in college, I tried dating a young woman whom my roommate was dating. When someone else actually said she would like to date me, my response was always quick, "I'd hate to ruin our friendship."

I had no real desire for it to happen. I realize now that I pursued impossible relationships because my inner self knew that it would never work. I could only imagine a kiss at most. I did not want anything else at all. I do not want to mislead you and say that I never felt any attraction to women, but somehow, it never rang true with me.

The "benefit" of my confusion—and it was confusion—was that I remained celibate. This celibacy fueled my fundamentalist Christian tendencies and made me even more self-righteous and pure. My homophobic and anti-choice stances flourished, and I buried the crying child deep within myself. I remembered that two young men in my high school were rumored to be gay. One of them had been a good friend in junior high. I was one of the worst taunters, condemners, and gossipers about them. I could not believe that they would even consider such actions. But at the same time that I was condemning them, I felt a deep interest in their lives together. I so desperately wanted to let my guard down and share my struggle, share my interest in men. But my youth directors, my pastors, my family, and especially my own rigid mind-set, said that homosexuality was the work of the devil, wrong and disgusting. I knew I was a Christian, and I would not be "disgusting" and "sinful."

What is almost shocking to me in retrospect is that during this period in my life, while I sat rather well in the judgment seat in my public life of righteousness and purity, I also lived a secret interior life. During my seventh grade year, I accidentally discovered some *Playboy* magazines. I read them whenever I had the chance. One day I realized that I spent very little time gazing at the women in the magazines; I was far more interested in the men. Later, I found the gift of a lifetime, the actual answer to what I had literally prayed for, a *Playgirl*. I loved it as I gazed over the naked bodies of bronzed men. It was certainly heaven. So while I condemned others in public, I had now begun in private to explore the possibility of loving men—but that could not be.

During these years, I found myself praying to God to heal me, to rid me of this great sin. I would pledge never again to read those magazines or masturbate to male fantasies, but they would almost cry out to me with a severe loudness. I promised God I would never lust after another guy in my classes, but inevitably I would find myself staring or daydreaming about a senior guy in my health class or my Texas history teacher. Then I would cycle through extreme anger, sadness, and guilt. I remember so many times getting on my knees in the bathroom and telling God what a horrible, pitiful person I was, and that I did not deserve to live. I was trash. I even worried that Satan had possessed me. I prayed and prayed. I committed myself to leading worship at the evening service at the church and served on committees, read scripture, and led the youth officers. The desires, however, did not go away. My workaholism flourished, and I committed myself to everything at school and everywhere else. I wrote pious sounding "God and America" letters to the city newspaper. I even said in my senior annual that all the world's problems could be solved by just returning to the Bible. I lived life with an almost split personality, and the church accepted without question the outward facade, in fact, they loved me. The little old ladies at the church would say, "James, you will make such a great preacher some day." The outer me was great, but underneath the pats and the love, cried a lonely child who felt worthless and hopeless. I genuinely wanted to serve God, but how could I, with such a sinful nature?

In this struggle, I graduated from high school, and I really began to question my place in the world, my need to be in the church or even to live. My freshman year in college was a living hell, trying so hard to be a good Baptist boy, and hurting so badly inside my soul. The sad thing was that the Church and its numerous ministries were not and could not be there for me. I feared them so much. If anyone ever knew my struggle, it would be over. It seemed there was no reason to keep living. Thank God I ended up in a United Methodist Church. I had not yet fully come to the understanding that I was gay, but I did realize that I needed something. It was the United Methodist church that I now attended and its pastor who finally began to say, "You are okay." My memories of discovering a "liberal" James Preston, an open-minded person who loved to have fun and break down barriers, are wonderful. It was here that Communion and Baptism finally had meaning for me, where bread and wine and water meant grace and justice. It was here that healing and the labor of birth began.

I left that congregation to go to seminary, to answer God's call and to really be myself. I did not realize the day I arrived in Dallas that my call was an unfinished story. It had only begun, for it would be within the walls of the Perkins School of Theology at Southern Methodist University that I would hear God's call to quit lying to myself and others. I would finally come out, at least to a few close friends, as a gay Christian man. It would be (and still is) painful, but it was the most liberating step I have ever taken in my life. Coming out, in itself, was like a new baptism, for a new creature was born. I was reborn through the waters of honesty, love, and justice.

It was this new birth experience that also opened my eyes to the reality of the United Methodist Church and its pastors. As I came out to more persons and as I came out more fully to myself, I suddenly realized that even though the United Methodist Church had done so much for me, this denomination also was my oppressor. The United Methodist Church wore different clothing than the former churches that wore the coats and gloves of literal interpretation and condemnation to the fiery pits of hell. But it *did*, however, wear the gowns and tuxedos of silence, marginalization, and indifference and honored the sin of maintaining the status quo. Unfortunately my full realization of this truth came after I had been named an elder in the ordained ministry of the United Methodist Church.

As the truth of my oppression, even in the liberal congregation in which I now serve, becomes more visible and clear to me, I feel angry—really angry. I also feel abandoned and discouraged. The one place that I chose as a place of safety and full acceptance is no longer that place at all, but it is actually as hostile as the dual life and faith I lived as a youth. The day I finally realized that the United Methodist Church was against me was a day of deep depression and sadness. I remember just suddenly realizing that there was no longer any reason for me to remain in the denomination. It would not change its stance prohibiting the ordination of homosexuals any time soon and the well-intentioned but false promises of clergy and laity hurt as well. I cried for a long time that day because I did not want to leave. I do not want to leave the church that I chose nor leave the heritage and a community that in some ways brought me liberation and freedom. Yet to stay means facing lies, injustice, silence, marginalization, self-deception, and denial of my complete humanity, which have no place in the Church's mission or purpose. I do not want to find myself at age fifty still waiting like so many other gay and lesbian clergy whose eyes and expressions seem so lifeless. They have bought into an institutional lie, and they see no way out except through death.

My sense of fragmentation has led me to reconsider the meanings implicit in the sacraments. To offer or receive Communion seems almost hypocritical because I cannot offer my complete self at the rail. I wept openly the day that I was able to go to the rail at the Cathedral of Hope Metropolitan Community Church in Dallas and say, "My name is James, and I'm gay!" I received the body and blood of Christ as my full self, truly "Just As I Am," and the reality of my baptism was made complete. As this year passes by, I realize that my days as a pastor in the United Methodist Church are numbered. I do feel pain, but underneath the struggle and the fear is a baptized child of God no longer wanting to be dis-membered in his living and his loving.

MARK

I have been putting off doing this for as long as I could, and I never allowed myself to wonder why. Now it's quite difficult to know where to begin. . . .

My parents met and married in an Assemblies of God Pentecostal Church. It was such a church that I attended from infancy until about the age of seventeen.

My memories of it are as follows: the church was always warm and friendly. People were pleased to see you, and welcomed you. It was a happy place. People sang the hymns and choruses with great enthusiasm and spirit. The liturgy was very informal. Basically each service was improvised, led by the Spirit. Glossolalia was very prominent; speaking in tongues was to be heard in virtually every service, and most church members—including myself—practiced it. The theology of the Assemblies of God is fundamentalist, not to say that every word in the Bible is interpreted literally, but in the sense that scripture was the ultimate and sufficient authority on everything.

Naturally, until my teenage years I accepted my parents and the church's teaching on everything. I was "born again" at age eight, baptized (by immersion) in water at age nine, and "baptized in the spirit" (meaning I began to speak in tongues) at age ten. Incidentally, my parents were opposed to my water baptism and wanted me to wait, but such was the strength of my faith and conviction—or bloody-mindedness, if you prefer—that I had to have it done as soon as possible. I partook of the bread and wine for as long as I can remember; Pentecostals have a very "low" view of its significance.

The church we attended in Nottingham (we moved to Newark when I was about eleven) had a youth leader, Steve, whom I always declared to be my "favorite man." I found out recently that he was gay (and celibate—a missionary).

The Assemblies of God's position on homosexuality—as I remember it—is that sex between men is an abominable sin and that the homosexual movement is part of Satan's work. Homophobia was often expressed from the pulpit. I even read an article once which examined the notion that homosexuality was "the unforgivable sin."

I suppose I was about thirteen when I was first consciously attracted to other men. I still thought this had nothing to do with homosexuality or homosexuals, who were horrible, evil people. When I was fifteen, I had what could be loosely described as an affair with a man in the church. He was twenty-three, the age I am now. It was never physical, but certainly more than platonic. (What an ironic word in these circumstances!) After this came to an end, I faced up to the possibility that I could be gay. My faith was still very strong at this point. I wanted to go to Bible college and become a pastor. I used to get picked on at school for my faith, but that merely made it stronger. I used to enjoy feeling "different" from everyone else. Now I was beginning to wonder what my difference was.

From reading my Bible, it became quite clear to me what the situation was. My homosexual desires were a test, part of the "refining by fire" which is a part of every Christian's life. What I had to do then was written down on January 1st of my 1986 diary in two of my New Year's resolutions: (1) I will become completely heterosexual and (2) I will pray and read my Bible more often. God was challenging me in order to make my faith stronger. I was *privileged*. No one knew at this time what I was thinking or feeling; it was all a huge secret.

The next nine months were hell. It's interesting to wonder if they would have been different had I discovered masturbation (which I didn't for another year or so), as I'd never had any teaching to make me feel guilty about it. I'm still angry about this period of my life, and I don't know what to do with all the anger, hurt, and bitterness I feel. I was utterly alone, trying to make sense of everything, trying to salvage something from everything my reasons for living were based on, trying to fancy women, trying not to look at men or think about them, trying to be someone else, and trying to be myself. I don't know how to describe this very well, but I can feel my hand shaking and my insides shaking even as I try to write about it. I still don't feel that I've spoken to anyone who understands it, but I can't get it out of my system.

One good thing was happening to me at this time. Thanks to my piano teacher (who is still a wonderful friend), I was introduced to high Anglicanism. So much about it appealed (appeals) to me. First, the music. The sound of the choir and the organ affected me in a way that no other music did. The repertoire of Howells, Leighton, Harris, Purcell, Byrd, and Tallis moved me in an indescribable way. Secondly, I loved the coldness, the anonymity of Anglican worship. I no longer felt implicated in what I was doing or saying. It is all addressed to a very remote God who is unchanging. Pentecostals are highly charged emotionally and incontinent. There is a great personal focus on *me: my* life, *my* faith, *my* revelation, *my* God. *I* seemed totally irrelevant in a great building with a great history filled with great music, and that is very comforting.

In September 1986, I let go of everything and decided to fight no more. If I was gay (and I am) then so be it. I came out to my brother a few months later, and he was (and still is) completely fantastic. Over the next year my faith withered. I left the Pentecostal church and was appointed Assistant Organist at Newark Parish Church, a large high Anglican church. I was confirmed an Anglican, knowing that I had no faith.

"Coming out" at university was a wonderfully liberating experience. I played the organ in chapel and ran the chapel choir. I seem to have a little talent in this area and it's something I want to keep doing.

After graduation, I went to be organist at First United Methodist Church in Lubbock, Texas. Living in the "Bible belt" and being surrounded by Christians—ones of quite an active faith—stirred up many of my experiences and problems of the past. For example, the rather public way in which this church took communion—it is brought around to your seat—is rather more threatening than the Anglican anonymity, where you can sit and watch if you like, without drawing any attention to yourself.

I felt quite alienated by all of this, and yet , in a way, I wanted to become part of it again. I have done a lot of reading around the subjects of faith, theology, the historical Jesus, and so on, in order to find out what I can salvage, if anything, of my faith. In a way, I'd quite like to break from the church completely and forget it all. I wish I didn't remember being baptized. I wish I didn't play the organ and love church music, sometimes.

Really, I don't know where to go from here.

2 ♦ Silenced: Stories of Exclusion and Pain

Almost every Sunday morning finds me, along with other brothers and sisters in Christ, coming to the altar rail of a church to receive the sacrament of Holy Communion. At this rail I kneel and offer my prayers and my reflections. At this construction of poles and railings I patiently wait to be served, to offer myself and my gifts in thanksgiving in response to the grace of God. My senior pastor comes my way; I place my hands out and I offer my name, "James." I then find bread in my hand to be dipped in the passing cup. Yet I realize as I chew this wine-soaked bread that in truth I have not offered myself totally in this exercise of grace and justice. The bread and wine are really transformed into my blood and my body sacrificed because of a deep silence—a forced silence mandated by many of the men and women who kneel with me each Sunday.

These fellow Christians along the rail do not truly know my full personhood. They can tell you that I am their associate pastor, that I love and work with their youth. They can even tell you how I was called to ministry in this church. This congregation can tell you my parents' names, my favorite music group, my favorite food, but these friends in the faith cannot tell you that I am gay—that I am a homosexual Christian man. It would be impossible for some to accept. Even though some suspect my homosexuality, they do not want to know about the real me. Some want me to keep quiet, to remain silent. As I look down that long row of faces, I also realize that several of them are lesbian and gay, and they too are silenced. These lesbian women and gay men are dis-membered from the body of Christ by fear and prejudice.

How We Are Silenced—Why We Are Silenced

Gays and lesbians are silenced by the hatred and fear of the society in which we live, the fears of the families into which we were born, and the institutionalized prejudice of the Church, which at one time pledged to nurture and support. Gay and lesbian people are also silenced by their own self-hatred, fear, and prejudice. Gay and lesbian Christians are silenced by homophobia. Writer and activist Suzanne Pharr defines "homophobia" as "the irrational fear and hatred of those who love and sexually desire those of the same sex."[1] This fear and hatred are what very often seal the lips of lesbian and gay Christians. They know the possible results of ending silence. They know that to "come out" may mean rejection by friends, loss of employment, threats against their life, and banishment from their families. They can see the possibilities of losing children, being beaten or bashed, suffering rape, losing life—losing everything. Homophobia does an excellent job of silencing gays/lesbians, and it also keeps non-gays and non-lesbians trapped, unable to move beyond their own fears.[2] It is this life of silence that is continually reinforced and undergirded by the Church, and it is this life of silence that brings so much pain.

It is not as though my sexuality and sexual orientation are minor parts of my life or of the lives of the many gay and lesbian Christians throughout the Church. My homosexuality is a major component of my being. It is my sexuality—a major part of my identity, my living, and my life. My sexuality is so tightly woven into the fabric of my spirituality as a Christian that I cannot separate it. And yet the Church says I must be silent and hide a part of the image of God that is reflected in me. I am fearfully and wonderfully made as a sexual being, yet many Sundays, that communion rail becomes a prison wall, with bars and barbs enclosing my complete self in a silent cell. As gay and lesbian Christians come forward to experience God's grace and justice, they in turn receive an understood command, "Be silent. Do not tell us who you are. We do not want to know." Our lips are sealed, our open hands are closed, and our hearts are broken—because of the fear, rejection, hatred, and homophobia of the Church of Jesus Christ.

The Manifestations of Being Silenced

The silencing of lesbian and gay Christians is still the norm in the Church. I assume that some mainline Christians are aware that their gay brothers and lesbian sisters are living as silenced people, barely connected by fragile threads to the body of Christ. Certainly, others are not willing to admit that gays and lesbians are even in the Church. And now, especially in light of the recent compromise concerning lesbians and gays in our military, I would guess that most mainline Christians would adhere to the belief that silence is not a horrible thing. In fact, they may even believe silence is a better alternative to the possible persecution and hatred that results from being completely out as a homosexual Christian. Unfortunately, this belief is where the Church ironically commits a sin against gay and lesbian Christians.

In reality, silencing is neither effective nor acceptable, because the pain and oppression of gay/lesbian Christians cannot truly be silenced. Shame and guilt cannot completely silence a people. They will cry out in their pain and agony. Recall how Habakkuk addressed the acts of the wicked nations in chapter 2,

> You have devised shame for
>   your house
>   by cutting off many peoples;
>   you have forfeited your life.
> The very stones will cry out
>   from the wall,
>   and the plaster will respond
>   from the woodwork.
>   (Hab. 2:10–11)

As Habakkuk reminds us, people cannot truly be silenced. The hurt and longing of lesbian and gay people will find a way to be heard. These intense aches and cries will find ways to escape through the cracks in the tombs of silence. The results of silencing are often more painful, more dangerous, and even more life-threatening than the feelings that gave them birth.

The Church must realize that shameful silence produces a distorted image of God, the body of Christ, and of oneself, a dysfunctional search for intimacy, an entrapment of ordination, and many times, a complete exit from the Church. The Church's act of silencing lesbians and gays is not a passive or benevolent act of love. In silencing the complete selfhood of gay/lesbian Christians, the Church obstructs their full participation in the body of Christ.

A Distorted Image of God and Self

The pain of silence actually starts in our beginnings. We were born, made, in the image of our Creator (*imago dei*). As Joseph L. Allen states,

The apex of the "imago dei" is then the capacity for covenant
. . . an essential feature, created by God, through which each
person individually, irreplaceably, and equally has worth as
an end, and not only as a means. Out of love, God creates us
capable of entering into covenant and capable then of mir-
roring God. This is to say that God creates us for steadfast
community with God and with one another.[3]

Genesis 1:27, 31 states:

So God created humankind in
    his image,
    in the image of God, he created
    them;
    male and female he created
    them.
. . . .
God saw everything that he had made,
and indeed, it was very good.

We were created in God's image, reflections of our Creator in the
fullness of our humanity as sexual and spiritual beings. We were also
created good, and yet from the beginning, especially once we realized
that we were different from many others, we heard both blatant and
submerged notions of how bad we actually were. From the very beginning of our childhood, showing any signs of loving a person of the
same sex triggered alarms in our families and teachers. We were encouraged to do "boy" or "girl" things. We heard directly and indirectly the negative comments about "tomboys" and "sissies," and we
knew we did not want those labels. Of course, it was far worse for a
boy to be thought of as a "sissy" than a girl to be a "tomboy," for
"masculine" traits in any form were always more highly valued. The
problem with being a "sissy" was that a boy "lowered" himself to act
like a girl. A parallel for girls would be today's negative term "butch."
To be "butch" means a woman crosses the line of femininity and dis-
regards her need for a man.[4] In response, we internalized and buried
our sexuality—we were silenced. A very basic part of ourselves was
locked away. As later years approached, the commands for our silence became more direct in the homophobic words of our classmates, our parents, our friends, and our church.

    I remember hearing the negative words spoken about my father's
"Queer" cousin just as I, a junior high school boy, was falling in love
with the man in the lead part of an outdoor drama my family had recently attended. How could I love this beautiful man and fantasize

about him if it were so bad? I prayed and prayed that my feelings and attraction would stop. I often questioned my faith as I thumbed to his picture in the program book that we had taken home. The direct and indirect silencing made me doubt my baptism—God's claim on me.

Several years before, after completing membership training in my local Baptist church, I decided as a nine-year-old boy that it was time to be baptized. The day was marked by the congregation voting to accept me into church membership and approving my desire to be baptized. As a United Methodist Christian, I realize a vote was not necessary for my baptism. God acted and claimed me in that moment. Yet that vote was almost identical to the pledge made by mainline Christians at baptism, "We will love and nurture this person." What joy I felt as my local church family voted me into the body of Christ! What pain I felt later as the church quickly moved to silence me with their homophobia. "We really do not want you to be who you are," they seemed to say.

Only much later, as I came to terms with being gay, did I realize the blasphemy of both the Baptist congregation that baptized me and the United Methodist Church that I still serve as a clergy person. To silence me and call me unworthy of God's love and grace is a breach of the baptismal covenant. The Church attempts to silence God's prophetic call when they silence the baptized gay or lesbian Christian. The results of such silencing are deep, bleeding wounds and a life lived in the darkest and most hopeless places. We are silenced by the Church's homophobia only to be driven into adult bookstores, self-destructive behaviors, abusive relationships, or the deafening silence of the closet. We are too afraid to speak out, to reveal ourselves, or to share our love for the same sex. We are too fearful that our ministries will be stopped, our jobs will be lost, our place in the body of Christ will no longer exist. The Church, in silencing the gay and lesbian child of God, makes the Communion rail a prison and the waters of baptism a whirlpool of death because it sends the gay and lesbian out of the Church believing they are less than children of God.

The Church also imprisons itself with a lack of wholeness and an environment of deceit and lies. As Paul states in 1 Corinthians 12, "all the members of the body, though many, are one body, so it is with Christ. . . . If one member suffers, all suffer together with it; if one member is honored, all rejoice together with it." By estranging or silencing lesbian women and gay men, the Church silences or cuts off part of itself, limiting its scope and vision. Gifts, graces, and opportunities to seek God's world are lost. The community of faith is incomplete—broken—and does not resemble the vital, diverse body Christ calls us to be. It also becomes a place where secrets are kept, where pain and hurt are buried deep within the souls of those who are in the pews. Parents, friends, and family of gay/lesbian Christians, as well as the gay men and lesbian women themselves, are not permitted to share their joys or their sufferings but are encouraged to lie and hide.

Even more frustrating to the gay or lesbian Christian in the mainline or liberal/moderate church is the two-faced, weak-willed approach, which appears more tolerable at first, but in reality, is the same painful rejection that comes from other segments of Christianity. Within this understanding of Christianity the battle of the homosexual Christian's place is fierce and very painful. Within this realm we hear words like those of one denomination's official stance:

> Homosexual persons no less than heterosexual persons are individuals of sacred worth. All persons need the ministry and guidance of the Church in their struggles for human fulfillment, as well as the spiritual and emotional care of a fellowship which enables reconciling relationships with God, with others, and with self. Although we do not condone the practice of homosexuality and consider this practice incompatible with Christian teaching, we affirm that God's grace is available to all. . . .[5]

"Incompatible with Christian teaching." . . . "Persons of sacred worth?" . . . How can those phrases be in the same statement? How can a church of Jesus Christ say that we are incompatible with the faith and then at the same time call us persons of sacred value? Thank you, but no thank you. This statement is a prime example of the attitude of clergy and lay people alike within the mainline church. It is a middle-of-the-road, ride-the-fence approach to the liberation of homosexual Christians. It is an easy way of wording the situation so that the Church eases the consciences of the more compassionate while it fuels the fires of the more homophobic. The heartbreaking part about this approach is that it silences gay and lesbians each day by saying, "We love you, but we do not think you are compatible; We love you, but we do not want to truly know you." It is no more compassionate than outright rejection. In fact, it may be more painful. It is an approach to homosexuality that uses people's talents and gifts for the church, but does not allow them to live truthfully.

This silence hurts, severs, and, in fact, degrades gay/lesbian Christians every day. This hypocritical silence instills fear and creates isolation for gays and lesbians. It also keeps younger lesbian women and gay men from finding good positive role models. The inability to speak the truth slowly destroys the very basic foundation of the Church as a place of honesty and truth-telling. It, like the world around it, becomes nothing but an intricate network of lies, secrets, and hatred. The Church's act of silencing is a powerful sin, especially within the context of the deeply rooted sacramental theology found in most mainline churches.

A Distorted View of the Body of Christ and Our Place In It

Recently, I was a part of a Bible study training course within my denomination. One evening as a group of us ate dinner, an associate pastor from West Texas said that "these modern issues" of homosexuality, the environment, and abortion were somewhat important, but they were too often the object of discussion for our denomination. He said, "the average man in the pew does not care at all about these things. He's just trying to live day to day. Sure, these issues should be talked about, but we talk about them too much. They really are not that relevant." This pastor's comments are another example of silencing—locking the door on people's lives.

Again, a mainline clergy person contributes to the silencing of many within the Church, including many of his own parishioners. This pastor assumes that no one in *his* congregation has had an abortion or has seen the earth's destruction and felt fear. It does not cross his mind that at that very moment at *his* table, there sat at least one homosexual Christian man who definitely thinks the issue of gay liberation in the Church is a critical issue. He could not have fathomed that this gay man could not even speak one word for fear of being revealed, outed, chastised, criticized, and destroyed. He, in his great concern for pastoring the "average man," cut deeper the wound of rejection and pain.

How many lesbian and gay Christians hear these same silencing words every Sunday from their pastors and their laity? How often do fence-riding Christians assume that no gays or lesbians could even be in their midst? How often do they say and do things that bury the sexuality and spirituality of homosexual Christians deeper, often severing hope and grace from many persons? I would like to say to that "pastorally concerned" associate pastor that his remarks are ignorant and self-centered—far from the call of Christ to love our neighbor. In fact, what that pastor is really saying is that these issues are not relevant to him, therefore they must not be relevant for local congregations, for presbyteries, for associations, for conferences or for other judicatory bodies. And while he makes these grand assessments of the average person in the pew, real people with real feelings—gays, lesbians, our families, and our friends—sit in the pews each Sunday and either hear the indifference or the negation of our lifestyles or the lifestyles of those we love. We, as baptized, faithful children of God, cannot speak. We cannot counteract the ignorance uttered from the mouths of pastors who often promote patriarchal beliefs with their good intentions. We cannot speak because we are afraid we will no longer be welcome. We cannot speak because we fear our families or we, ourselves, will be rejected. We cannot speak because we too begin to question the fact that we are baptized children of God, worthy of Holy Communion. We cannot tell our story because we are frightened that our ordination will be revoked, and we will no longer be able to answer fully God's call to ordained ministry. We cannot speak because we are afraid of physical harm. We cannot say anything because mainline Christian people will not stand up and be advocates for the liberation of their gay sisters and brothers.

The Church in all its glory has convinced us that to express a major part of our created selves would be a terrible sin. The Church encourages us to remain silent in the tension of the sacred and the incompatible, and if we will follow the rules, we will be taken care of and conditionally be accepted. Yet we all know that silence kills and destroys. It is a slow process of death, for no life springs forth from the grave of silence. I say to mainline pastors who continue to "wait and see" about this homosexual issue, "Are you, my sister, my brother, truly within the bounds of the Christian faith? Are you really following the teachings of Christ? Have you succumbed to blasphemy?"

Silencing the voices of the oppressed works like a thunderstorm, towering over the land below, bringing turbulent winds, pelting rain, piercing hail, booming thunder, and sharp bolts of lightning, causing the people to run to shelter below the earth, in cellars, where they can neither be seen nor heard. Silencing destroys dreams and provides fertile ground for resentment about the church, about God, and even about self. Resentment grows into anger and possibly rage. Long-term silence points to the hopelessness of a deeply ingrained oppression that seems so powerful and that weaves itself into every fabric of our living. The silencing of lesbian and gay Christians by their church is often detrimental and deadly, and unfortunately it is reinforced every day when the covenant of Baptism and the liberation of Communion are restricted or canceled. This silence often causes or leads gay and lesbian persons to self-destructive behavior because we begin to believe that we are less than children of God— less than human. We do not believe that we are worthy of love, or sometimes of life.

The Dysfunctional Search for Intimacy and the Growth of Rage

It is the Church's act of silencing that often sends gays/lesbians into situations that compromise our integrity, destroy our self-image, and often threaten our very lives. Certainly, gays/lesbians make the choices to enter into these dark and hopeless situations, but when doors are shut in your face, even the ornate doors of the Church, one often collapses in exhaustion and settles for the fear, the pain, and the risk. One young man's story exemplifies this tragedy.

> I have walked into dark and hopeless places because of my inability to live openly as a gay man. I make no excuses for my "sin," but often my situation does seem hopeless. It is dark and scary within these places, risky and dangerous. It is within the walls of these places that I feel insulted; I know God is insulted. It is within these bookstores, these parks, these restrooms that men meet to hold each other, to caress, to have sex, to love, and to hate. Sometimes, you encounter someone who will kiss you, someone who is more interested in you than what your body can do for them. Someone who actually sees your face, touches your cheek, hugs you so tightly that tears well up in the darkness of this prison. It is these men who are sacramental to me, who have provided glimpses of grace for my whole self. And yet it is only a glimpse of light in these pits of hell. For they, like me, have waited so long to feel the love that the Church forbids—the love of a man.
>
> I met my first lover in one of these pits of hell. He was the

first man, the first complete affirmation of my homosexuality. Thank God that we left that dark and fearful place for our time together. As he began to hold me and touch me, my whole body and soul shook and spasmed as the freedom flowed. As we kissed and caressed, I felt that I had become a living, breathing, pulsating, sexual prayer to God. It was a spiritual experience that celebrated my reflective nature of God.

And yet, for the few times that I have found glimpses of grace in those pits, there have been other times that the silencing has brought me to deeper places that cried of disgust and death. There have been times that I have felt nothing like a reflection of God, and more like the darkest and most dreaded creation of all the earth. As I have listened to video screams and watched nervous pacing, I have felt that God has left me, abandoned me to be swallowed by the depths of which the psalmists speak. It was there in those horrible places that I subjected myself to abuse, fear, force, and pain. It was then that I no longer believed in myself nor saw the image of God anymore.

From a gay man, name withheld

Gays and lesbians feel so much rage in the face of these tombs. So many gays and lesbians realize that the Church, the body of Christ, sends them into horrible situations, without hope, without the resurrection. How terribly sad it is that the Church brings such hurt and pain to gay and lesbian Christians. The Church relegates them and so many others to lives without wholeness, smiles, real love, and filled with only empty stares, unknown partners, lonely nights, fearful walks, darkened spaces, and isolated places.

Here, in these places, the church commits its sin. Here the silence toward liberation of lesbian and gay Christians buries God's children with shame and guilt. Here, crucifixion is alive and well. Could it be that the Church's choice to remain silent and to allow the sin of homophobia to go unchallenged causes suffering and pain for gays/lesbians? When Esther seemed to waver in her efforts to combat the sin of Haman, Mordecai said to her, "Do not think that in the king's palace you will escape any more than all the other Jews. For if you keep silence at such a time as this, relief and deliverance will rise for the Jews from another quarter, but you and your father's family will perish" (Esth. 4:13–14). The Church's own silence and its unwillingness to listen to the voices of gay and lesbian persons will compromise the Church and its mission. Like Esther, God calls the Church to stand in solidarity, working toward the liberation of oppressed peoples, in a place of honesty and integrity. That mission is desecrated when the Church either stands by idly as people suffer from the homophobia of the world (and of the Church itself) or are made to live incomplete lives, silencing a portion of their created self. The church becomes a place of unrighteousness and injustice.

The silencing also leads lesbian and gay Christians to other deadly and hopeless situations. Suicide is a major problem within the lesbian and gay community. A study by Jay and Young determined that 40 percent of the gay men and 39 percent of the lesbian women surveyed had either attempted or seriously contemplated suicide.[6] A similar finding in a study by Bell and Weinberg found 35 percent of the gay men and 38 percent of the lesbian women surveyed had either seriously considered or attempted suicide.[6] When gay and lesbian people feel that they are not worthy of love and acceptance by their colleagues, friends, or family because of their sexual orientation, they in turn question the validity of their own lives. When they realize that a life image of their own or of their family cannot be fulfilled because of their orientation, they often feel hopeless about the future, and depressed about their lives.[7] We, as homosexual Christians, do not find the affirmation of our goodness or our very existence, in the Church. Therefore, we sometimes question why we should continue to live a life of silence, torment, and hopelessness.

Unfortunately, the issue of suicide is worse among gay and lesbian youth. According to the "Report of the Secretary's Task Force on Youth Suicide," suicide is the leading cause of death among gay, lesbian, bisexual, and transsexual youth. Gay and lesbian youth are two to three times more likely to attempt suicide than their heterosexual counterparts, and in fact, gay/lesbian youth suicides may comprise up to 30 percent of the completed youth suicides annually. One of the many factors in suicide is difficulty in self-acceptance due to negative self-image and a feeling of total isolation.[8] Religion also is a major factor in creating an environment for suicide attempts by lesbian and gay youth. Their faith may misinform their family about homosexuality, resulting in isolation, rejection, hatred, and even eviction from the home. Their religion may also label them as wicked and condemned to hell, which creates a variety of internal conflict for the faithful lesbian or gay youth. The option that may often come to mind for the gay or lesbian youth is suicide.[9] How many youth in our Church's youth groups and fellowships cannot be themselves? How many live in fear and isolation? How many suicides in our churches by young men and women have really been caused by the homophobia of the Church? The Church kills even the children within its walls—the children of God who are lesbian and gay.

The Entrapment of Ordination

The call by God to specialized or ordained ministry can often complicate the gay/lesbian struggle within the Church. In my own coming out process, my call to ordained ministry in the United Methodist Church has been challenged and questioned at every turn. I struggled with this call from God for many years, finally responding and going to seminary. Yet it was in the midst of fulfilling the requirements for my service as an ordained clergy person that I realized my whole self: a gay Christian man. Especially during the initial revelation of my homosexuality, I cried to God, "What sick joke is this? God, You got me here, and now You want to see me get kicked out." Only later in my journey did I realize that my calling to ministry is *very* valid, and so is my sexual identity. In fact, I believe both are vital components of a larger journey to which God has called me.

The potential danger of ordination or specialized ministry is that it very often acts as a trap. Many gays/lesbians are convinced that if they can make it through the hoops of interviews, doctrinal papers, sermons, tests, and the voting, they will be fine. For many gay and lesbian clergy, some sort of fantasy exists that full acceptance and living openly will be found on the other side of the ordination process. I know in my own journey I believed that I could prove myself and my calling to the Church, and that once I completed all of the requirements, I would be making this powerful profession of liberation. What I later realized—on the night of my ordination as an elder in the United Methodist Church—was a deep sense of depression and regret. I had misled myself about the Church's attitude toward gays/lesbians and now my gifts and talents could be completely "exploited." I would only need to remain silent, closeted, and repressed to continue to receive the Church's approval and acceptance.

Gays/Lesbians are entrapped throughout the Church as they wear their stoles, wrap themselves in their white albs, and don their collars. Many are waiting for a liberation that may never come from an institution that has long preferred silence over truth. As lesbian and gay clergy, we cannot continue to work harder to prove ourselves; it will only kill us. We must liberate ourselves and call the Church to lift its shroud of silence. That is our gift to the Church.

A Call to Cease the Silencing

The Church must call for our liberation, not our crucifixion. At junior-high church camp one summer, we reenacted the crucifixion of Jesus. The soldiers entered one of our nightly worship services and began to flog the character of Jesus, played by a youth worker named Blake. Soon, all two-hundred campers were on their feet following Jesus to Calvary, a worship area about one-quarter of a mile away. All along the path sponsors and youth called out in their best theatrical effort, "Crucify him! Kill him! He deserves to die!" I along with others found myself really into the effort when I heard a different shout—a solo proclamation. "Save him, he's my friend. Save him. He should not die! Save him please!" And soon I saw him, Bear, a physically-challenged youth from Blake's youth group, running as fast as his body could take him, crying and calling "Save him!" I suddenly found myself whisked out of the theatrical and into the Holy. I suddenly did not want "Jesus" to die, to fall, to be hurt. I wanted him to be saved. I cried "Save him, please save him!"

It is time now for the Church—lay and clergy—to do just that. Gays/Lesbians need to be free in all places, especially within the community of faith. Suzanne Pharr states what she believes lesbians want, and in turn what I believe all homosexual Christians want.

> We want the elimination of homophobia. We are seeking equality. Equality that is more than tolerance, compassion, understanding, acceptance, benevolence, for these still come from a place of implied superiority: favors granted to those less fortunate. . . . The elimination of homophobia requires that homosexual identity be viewed as viable and legitimate and as normal as heterosexual identity. It does not require tolerance; it requires equal footing.[10]

Faithful Christians are called to run along the sides of a homophobic church full of hatred and remember the covenant the church made at the baptisms of hundreds of thousands. They must remember the grace and justice conveyed by Holy Communion and must run quickly and cry out, "Save them! Deliver our gay brothers and lesbian sisters! Stop betraying them and love them before the final nail is hammered and their spirits are destroyed. Put an end to this injustice, before you, the Church, destroy yourself." The Church cannot continue to silence gay and lesbian Christians along the journey, and it cannot continue to compromise itself as a place of righteousness and justice. Christians must hear the cries of gays and lesbians and respond with justice and grace. They must confess the sin of silencing present in the Church and lead the faith community toward a path of prophetic existence. The Church can really do no less if it is to truly be the sacramental body of Christ.

RICHARD

I remember, although not fondly, the earlier years of my life when church participation was an unbending requirement. Each and every Sunday with few exceptions, my parents, especially my mother, dragged me out of bed for Sunday school and church. At the time I did not resent the idea of church, per se, I just did not like the discipline of having to go repeatedly through what was to me a meaningless ritual.

I know now that the purpose of these early exposures to religion was to lay the foundation for a meaningful faith in God when I reached the age to truly appreciate His presence in my life. Unfortunately, by the time I was able to understand what the preachers were talking about, I had also realized that I plainly did not belong in their version of God's plan. For by that time, I knew I was gay.

I cannot recall the preachers ever directly mentioning homosexuality. I got the sense that it was such an egregious sin that it did not bear mentioning. The churches I attended were content to harp on the sins of their own members such as greed, lust, envy, etc. Since gay people were assumed to live exclusively in bohemian enclaves (quite unlike the Texas border town where I grew up), the wickedness of their ways was irrelevant. I have no doubt that had a gay been discovered in the church, homosexuality would have become very relevant very quickly.

I was confirmed in the Lutheran church at the age of thirteen. For several years I was compelled to attend classes on Tuesday nights in preparation for that event. I remember well many of the lessons, and to this day they still don't make any sense. The foundation underlying all of my religious education was the belief that all humans are inherently sinful and deserving of hell. That theme was often repeated. The church was intent on convincing us all that we were lost without the church's benevolent guidance to the path of glory.

That I needed guidance is without question. But early on, I doubted the church's benevolence. While much time and effort was devoted to pointing out all of the feelings, thoughts, and acts that could blot out God's light, little mention was given to the concept of God's love for us all. When it was mentioned, it was always in the context of how none of us deserved that love and that God was likely to withdraw it unless we toed the church line. My religious training left me with the distinct feeling that God was mad as hell and he was not going to take it much longer.

I continued going to church every Sunday until I left home for college. I can probably count my visits to church since that time on my fingers and toes, funerals excluded. My path to God took many drastic and unforeseen turns, but through the disasters of my life I have come to know God in a way the Church never made possible.

By the time I had reached the ripe age of twenty, I had developed a serious drinking problem. Actually, I didn't have much trouble drinking. It was the stopping part that gave me fits. For years I had tried to be as heterosexual as I possibly could. That effort took on two separate tacks. First, find a woman to become romantically involved with and eventually marry. Second, drink as much alcohol as necessary to make myself believe that I really enjoyed being romantically involved with women. Ironically, the alcohol struck the final blow in forcing me to face God and the truth.

I had finally reached a point where one of my woman schemes was beginning to work. But the bottle got in the way and I realized that I could not continue with the caper unless I sobered up. So I joined ranks with a band of recovering alcoholics who offered a path to sober living. I was horrified, however, when I learned that the path led directly to God. I could not fathom why God would want to help me, yet the drunks were explicit that He was my only hope. It was plain from my upbringing that God demanded a high toll for his favor.

The alcoholics held out a slim reed of hope. They told me that my understanding of God might not be entirely accurate. They also promised that if I honestly sought God and cleaned house, he would do for me what I could not do for myself. So I began my journey into a new life, joyous at the prospect of God removing the moral stains from my character. Finally, I would become the straight man that God wanted me to be. That my assumptions about God's expectations were inaccurate never really crossed my mind.

After several months of slogging through sober reality, I realized that my attraction to men had increased, not decreased. I became interested in a young man I had recently met, and I was devastated at my failure. I had done everything I was told to do with fervor. I had prayed and confessed and shared my innermost secrets with others, including my sexuality. And yet my gay feelings were stronger than they had ever been. What had I done wrong?

In a state of near panic I sought the advice of an alcoholic who had sobered up many years before me. He was a married, middle-aged man who apparently had seen it all. I told him in detail the shame of my failure and begged him to help me correct my sin. I wanted to be good. I wanted God's grace and love, but I didn't know how to get it.

My friend asked me if I chose to be gay. I told him no. I had nearly killed myself with drink trying to make it go away. He asked me if my family had made me gay. Again the answer was no. My family, especially my father, was quick to condemn homosexuality in any context. My friend then asked me if society had endeavored to make me gay. The answer was a firm no. I lived in constant fear of the ostracism that would follow if I were ever discovered. He then asked the question that I had never seriously considered before: "If all of these people did everything they could to keep you from being gay, and yet you are gay, who do you think made that happen? Who in this world has more power than every person in your life put together?"

The answer to the question was obvious. Yet my religious education and experience taught me to fight that truth with every last ounce of will I possessed. When faced with near certain self-destruction, I finally capitulated. That event occurred eight years ago. It was only a beginning, albeit a powerful one, of a new understanding of God. In being saved by a band of lowly drunks, I learned that God manifests himself in some truly unexpected ways. Along with that, I learned to be very careful in condemning others.

After seeing God through a new pair of glasses, I became very angry with religion. It became clear to me that the church is an ideal setting not for saving souls but for controlling minds. I realized that the word of humanity was often disguised as the word of God, with much human suffering as a result. But as soon as I decided to condemn religion universally, God began putting avid churchgoers into my life who were more interested in sharing God with me than in clubbing me with a Bible.

I do not attend any church at this time. While I now know that true Christian love exists, I haven't seen very much of it. I don't like the idea of going to a place and having to pretend I'm someone other than who I am. Many would call this a cop-out, an excuse for continuing inexcusable conduct. But I'm through wasting my life fighting God. If I am truly willing to follow Him, He will mark the path. And the path I see looks very different from what many people think it should look like. There may come a day when Christians will accept me as just another soul instead of a pathetic sinner needing condemnation or pity. Perhaps as God lifted the scales from my eyes eight years ago, he will again lift the scales and I will discover a new truth about those who call themselves Christians. Then again, it may work out the other way around.

MARIE

I was raised by two wonderful people. They were both loving, giving, and understanding. Everything they were was based on the Bible. My parents were in that Southern Baptist church every time the doors opened. As a matter of fact, they were there when the church was founded in 1961. They are still there today. So you can see that they are very strong in their beliefs. They did everything to instill their beliefs in their children. From the day I was born until I was about nineteen years old, I was involved in church; as a young child I learned nursery rhymes and Bible stories. When I got into my young teens, I became very involved. I participated in every activity—singing in the choir, playing trumpet solos for Sunday morning service, teaching Bible school in the summer, performing in plays, playing on softball teams, going to the old folks home. I participated in car washes, mountain retreats, and youth camp in the mountains of New Mexico. I was so immersed in church that there was no "me." Everything I did was to please my parents and my church. Somehow in my mind I knew that I was different, but I continued to please the church and ignore the self. I even went to Mexico two times on three-month trips as a singing missionary. My religion meant so much to me. I really could feel God and the love within His walls of protection.

When I got into high school, my parents felt that it was best to send me to a private school. I guess that is when my foundation started to shake. The school was run by an independent Baptist church. They not only wanted to educate me, but they also wanted to change my beliefs. They went to many extremes to rattle me. One day they called me a slut because I was wearing blue eye make-up and sitting next to a boy. Wow, that really pissed me off! So about a month later I decided to shock them. I held hands with my best friend as we walked down the hall. That really upset them. Needless to say, I had to change schools.

By this time I was sixteen years old and still had no idea that I was a lesbian. I knew that I was different but I didn't know how. The new school was also a strange experience. It was also a Christian school but it was called "Free Will." They spoke in tongues and did have a lot less rules than the other school. Mind you, through all of this I was still going to church with my parents, so I was getting two sets of rules for relating to God. That added to my internal confusion. What a struggle! During this time I had my first crush on another woman. I just didn't know what to call it, so I called it friendship. I had no other words to put on that feeling. Then one day she told me that she was moving. My world crashed! I became very bitter toward everyone and started to drift away from school, family, and church.

After graduation I went off to college, still not knowing that I was gay. I started going right away to the local Baptist church and to the Baptist Student Union. So you see, even after leaving my parents' nest I was still very grounded in my beliefs. I started going to all the events at the Baptist Student Union. At one of these events I was playing volleyball and I hit a very pretty young woman in the face with the ball. At the age of seventeen, I was about to learn more about myself and the church than in all my life.

This young woman and I moved in together as roommates. We went to church, school, Baptist Student Union, and home together. Neither one of us realized what we were. After a few months of sleeping together in the same bed, we both had many feelings that we did not act upon. One day she realized what we were, and soon we became lovers. All the missing pieces of my life came together. But as stories go . . .

We went to church on Sunday mornings and repented of our "sins" in tears, with all honesty, but by Sunday night we were back in bed. Yes, we were very troubled and confused. I just could not understand why God hated our love for each other. It was a love so strong and pure. What had we done to draw God's hate and disapproval?

Well, we went on like this for nine months. Then came summer break. She went off to California to be a summer missionary and I went to summer church camp to be a worker with kids. We were still together. After the summer we returned to college. She told me that she had slept with a Southern Baptist preacher man. I guess at that moment I knew somewhere someone was wrong about the kind of love I felt, because at least my love was an honest love. Even this preacher man had shown me that he didn't love his wife, his children, or his God

. . . because he had taken away my love. There were other people like him who ran me away from the church. One was the wife of my parents' preacher. She would follow me around and tell me that I was going to burn in hell for my lifestyle. She bothered my friends and my family. That really turned me off. She was acting as judge and jury over my life. Last year I came out, on my own, to my family. They of course threw the Bible at me. But they didn't put me out of their lives. At least the love of family held strong. . . .

GARY

"Look to your right. No not that far. Don't you see it. No the other way."

"Quick, get it before someone else sees it."

"Hurry. This way."

"I saw it first."

The grass in the side yard, barely beginning to show green, was alive with preschoolers intent on finding more Easter eggs than anyone else. I don't remember how many eggs I found that day, but it was enough to be rewarded with a small handkerchief covered with black and white kittens, which I kept for years. Looking back on it now, I'm sure everyone received something that day, but you hardly notice when you're five years old.

The thing I most remember about Sunday school is not the lessons or the teachers, but a glow in the dark disc with the face of Jesus on it. When I first received it, this circle of plastic was a great comfort to me, and I felt safe with it in my room, but as I grew older and became aware of my attraction to other men, it seemed to be looking down upon my bed, mentally chastising me through many a night of "impure desires."

Even in grade school, I walked a tightrope, trying to balance between what the Bible said were acceptable thoughts and what I was truly feeling. I prayed to the glow-in-the-dark plaque faithfully, but still the unacceptable thoughts and desires kept resurfacing.

I simply must not be trying hard enough to be good and pure, for everything was possible with Jesus, and so if I still had evil thoughts, it simply was that I wasn't concentrating enough and that I was totally to blame.

For as long as I can remember, my association with organized religion has been a love-hate relationship, a bittersweet roller-coaster ride with incredibly powerful highs and devastating lows.

I grew up in a town of approximately one hundred people in north-central Montana, where the only church we had was a small, picturesque Methodist church painted pristine white and located one-and-a-half blocks from the school.

My parents gave up on religion when I was four years old after a Catholic priest refused to bury the body of my three-year-old sister because my parents were not regular members of the congregation.

Even though they believed in God, my parents wanted no part of this, or any church, so religion was not a big part of my early life.

I attended Sunday school for a few years, but dropped that well before junior high. Then something curious and exciting happened in my junior year of high school. We got a new pastor who was interested in kids. For the first time ever, we had a church youth group. I went nervously to the meetings and decided that maybe this religion stuff wasn't so bad after all and that I probably hadn't given it a fair shake.

By this time, I had known for five or six years that I was a homosexual and was tormented by the Church's teachings that homosexuals are immoral, sinful, and surely doomed to hell. Well, who wants to be immoral, sinful, and doomed to hell? Certainly not me, especially when I was seventeen years old and afraid that even questioning the Bible meant a direct road to hell.

So imagine my ecstasy when a new preacher came and talked about the Bible in terms a seventeen-year-old could understand. He didn't mention homosexuality that I recall, but for the first time in a long, long while, church was fun.

It happened that this minister was deaning a church camp that year, and he encouraged me to be a counselor. Amid many self doubts, I decided to apply and was accepted for a camp of fifth- and sixth-graders. To say it changed my life would be a gross understatement. I was so enthralled by what happened at camp that year that I decided to dedicate my life to the church. I lived and breathed every breath for Jesus. Looking back I can only imagine how obnoxious I must have been, and if my parents were horrified by all this, they never let on.

Camp was in July, and in September of that same year, I moved to Denver to attend trade school. Sure, I still knew I was gay, and sure, I still knew the church condemned me, but I had made friends with Jesus, and he would make an exception for me. I vowed to find a church there and return to Montana every summer to counsel at camps for the remainder of my life.

But suddenly I found myself in a huge city surrounded by opportunities and stimulation I hadn't even known existed six months earlier. I tried a couple churches, but none of them were too exciting. Besides, there were so many other things to do on Sunday that eventually my commitment became as cold as the Colorado snow.

For the first time ever I was in a place where there were other gay people—people who looked and talked and acted like me. For the first time ever, I didn't feel like I was the only man in the world attracted to other men.

As liberating as it was just knowing they were there, I still could not bring myself to make contact with anyone or go to a bar or join a group. I was still being held hostage by the belief that homosexuality was wrong, sinful, and evil. So even though I was not in church every Sunday, the fear and the "God hates homos" belief that the church and society taught me were in me every day.

It was at this point that I decided I really didn't need the Church to be a good Christian and that if I prayed and lived right every day, surely God would provide me with all my desires.

So I focused all my efforts on living "right." I prayed faithfully every day and talked to Jesus morning, noon, and night. Of course, most of my conversations had to do with why I couldn't have the cute guy on the bus that morning or the man at the department store. (Was he really flirting with me, Jesus, or had I imagined it?)

Armed with passages such as "knock and the door shall be opened," "seek and ye shall find," "ask and it shall be given," I knew my perfect man would appear any day, totally sanctioned by God, and we would live happily ever after.

After several months of disappointment, I decided I must be doing something wrong, for the Bible says God takes care of his people and provides their every need. While it is true I had a place to live, food to eat, and a little money to spend, my needs were certainly not all being met.

The possibility that I might not be one of God's people because I was gay was too horrible to even think, so I thought the reason I wasn't finding love must have been because I wasn't going to church.

More than anything, I needed a place to say to me that I was a good person, loved and accepted unconditionally as a member of God's kingdom, regardless of my sexual orientation.

So I went back to church looking for such a place. Regrettably, what I found was a doctrine that said, "if you believe this way, live by a pre-scribed set of values, and study the prescribed set of readings, then you will be among the blessed. Anyone who believes something else belongs to some other faith." Unfortunately, I was in the latter group, or at least I thought so at the time.

So I spent the next ten years or so vacillating between no church connections at all and full membership as a widely known youth leader in one of the largest churches in the state.

All the while, I put the issue of my sexuality on the back burner and came to the belief that as long as I was not sexually active, it was okay to be gay. I could still reap the benefits the Bible promised.

I lived this fairy tale for several years, with the church at the center of my social life. In 1990, I decided to accept a job offer in Oregon. Off I went in search of greener pastures, leaving my church ties behind once again.

I'm not sure what was different, but slowly I found the need for love and acceptance being nudged into the foreground of my life again. Little by little I found I could no longer deny who I was.

For so many years I refused to acknowledge my attraction to other men simply because a group of people believing a certain doctrine said it was evil and sick. I finally knew I was not evil or sick, so instead of questioning myself and my beliefs, I began to question the beliefs of the church. This was not an easy or comfortable thing to do, since I like most people, had been taught never to question the Bible, for to do so was in itself evil and led to damnation.

After much thought, I decided that maybe an organization that thinks I am at best a second-rate citizen, is not where I want to spend my time and money after all. When I hear of congregations becoming "Reconciling," I am encouraged, but we still have a long way to go.

As long as the central governing body of the church says we will tolerate gays and welcome them into our church but we will not allow them to be preachers or teachers, it appears self-defeating for me to support that church. The limited tolerance and conditional acceptance the Church is offering seems to me to be a giant step backwards.

Have I given up on organized religion? I guess I have to say yes. I do not fit into their neat little box of people who are saved. There was a time I was dismayed by that. Today I celebrate it!

Have I given up on God? I guess I have to say yes . . . if you are referring to some male deity who abides beyond the sky with all the people who have lived acceptable lives on earth.

If you are speaking of a God who lives in everything, loves unconditionally without judging, and is a wonderful, ever-evolving mystery, I say I most definitely have not given up on God.

Where my spiritual journey leads me from here I do not know. I believe there are many paths to God, each one individually tailored and holy and valid. I can't say I'll never be involved in organized religion again, but until the Church unconditionally includes everyone, I will spend my time, energy, and money supporting places where I will be loved and accepted for who I am instead of for some narrow definition of who someone else thinks I should be.

3 ◆ Strangers: Stories of Judgment

"So then you are no longer strangers and aliens, but you are citizens with the saints and also members of the household of God. . . . "
—Eph. 2:19

"Oppression is not only evil, it is blasphemous because it makes a child of God doubt that s/he is a child of God."
—Archbishop Desmond Tutu

Dear Fitz,

You have seen and felt my pain, and you ask how you can help. You have already begun.

When I first came out as a lesbian to you, you were stunned. I know that you struggled to understand, but mostly you worked to absorb the surprise and shock. I did not fit the stereotypes, maybe? You had not expected that from me, maybe? No matter, I heard no judgments cross your lips and that helped me. I knew that our level of trust and care would transcend not having everything worked out in mind and heart.

A year later, you admitted your previous surprise and you told me that if I asked you to march for my rights as a citizen of this country and as a child of God that you would, no matter how reluctant you might still feel.

Another year passed and you witnessed for yourself the damage a blatantly disparaging song against gays can do. You felt the pain and sorrow with me; you stood up in protest when others sat in silence. You confronted those responsible by teaching them lessons from the heart. You told me that you would march anytime now without reservation. Your march had already begun.

Thank you for telling me that you understood that I wake up every day and have to live with the awareness that I am lesbian and, therefore, in many eyes, subhuman and substandard. You admitted that as a non-gay white man you can take for granted your identity. You get to be Fitz, plain and simple. You are judged by who you are as you, rather than as a credit or a curse to your gender, ethnic, or sexual-orientation group.

What is the difference between you—you who stood up for me, listened to me, and kept pushing the limits of your understanding—and those who refuse to grow? Was it our relationship of trust built over years of campfires that kept you engaged and growing? Was it because you had a live, flesh-and-blood person who kept coming up in your memory each time the word "lesbian" was spoken? For you the issue was not theoretical but embodied.

Fitz, I am totally frustrated with our denominational family who refuses to move from theoretical to personal. The conversations stay on such a detached level—on purpose, I suppose. Homophobia is so powerful and prevalent; it blocks movement. It hides behind the mask of "further study," or "it's just a joke," or "homosexuality is incompatible with Christian teaching."

Part of the problem is that many gay and lesbian Christians are frightened into silence. We want to worship fully, and we fool ourselves into thinking that we can leave part of ourselves outside the church doors and still fully participate. But how can we experience God's grace if we are holding back? Silence smothers. Silence isolates.

The alternative, though, is to be rejected in the House of Unconditional Love. Beyond the spiritual come the practicalities of financial survival, physical safety, and the protection of emotional boundaries.

How are we to move from theory to person if it is not safe for our faces to be shown? What are ways that safety can be nurtured?

I have seen some attempts at creating that sanctuary. One popular stance is to draw on the imagery and experience of the "stranger." Pastors preach to seemingly non-gay congregations about the command to offer protection and hospitality to the "stranger." "You shall not wrong or oppress a resident alien (stranger), for you were aliens in the land of Egypt" (Exod. 22:21). "You shall also love the stranger; for you were strangers in the land of Egypt" (Deut. 10:19).

Seems like a supportive argument on the surface; but it does little to move beyond the stereotypes, move beyond calling us outsiders and outcasts, dis-membering us from the body of Christ. Yes, clearly we are the outcasts in a homophobic society that fills the pews every Sunday, but within the walls of the church, who is in and who is not? Who are children of God and who are not? Who is the stranger here? Are we not all, as baptized Christians, children of God?

Does the pastor, out of sheer ignorance, assume that the people in the pews are all heterosexual and "in"? Have the gays and lesbians present kept their secret so successfully? No one suspects; no one knows them.

Is the pastor in denial about the presence of gays in the congregation? Would the pastor knowingly make such divisions from the pulpit: family, stranger. Would the pastor say, "Accept one another now; touch the untouchables."

Is there not an inherent judgment in the term "stranger"? To think of us as strangers is a product of heterosexist thinking: heterosexuality is the standard, all else is strange.

The "stranger" label still presents judgment. The label classifies one as being on the outside. But baptized gay and lesbian Christians have *already* been brought into the fold. We sit in the pews beside the non-gays and listen to the same sermons, cringing at the discrimination, hoping for a better world. . . .

Please keep on seeking justice.

Your friend,
Marilyn

Often the "good news" preached for gays/lesbians from the pulpits of moderate to liberal mainline churches is to name lesbian and gay people as the stranger, the outsider, or the Samaritan and thus always different from "us," but still worthy of love. This perspective assumes that the listeners are all heterosexual and that homosexuals are outside the church. If the silence (described in chapter 2) does not result in enough oppression, then lesbian and gay people are told that they are strange, plagued, and outside the walls of the church. This attitude, though an effort to move in the right direction, still serves the purpose of dis-membering and categorizing rather than re-membering and embracing.

This chapter will address biblical images of the stranger and the church's investment in heterosexism, sexism, erotophobia, and homophobia. It will also argue that the Church has an ethical responsibility in shaping gay/lesbian Christians' self-identity as children of God rather than as strangers. Stories that reflect multiple layers of estrangement (i.e., for homosexual and bisexual women, survivors of abuse, and ethnic minority persons) will be woven throughout the chapter.

Stranger or Estranged

Today we have conferences and councils that decide who are members of the body of Christ. Only those who obey Church law, they say. Only those who uphold traditional family values. Only those who agree with our ideology. Only those who are compatible with Christian teaching. No matter their personal commitment?, we may ask. No matter if they love Jesus? No matter if they seek the Christ as Lord and Savior? No matter if they follow the Nazarene's path of justice and mercy?

Who is the Church? Who makes up the body of Christ? Who decides?

These questions have been asked since the Church's beginning. Who belongs, who does not? Who builds us up, who tears us down? These are questions of identity and survival, protection of property and privilege. The lines are drawn; who is in, who is out? Who is familiar, who is the stranger?

A dictionary's definitions of the word *stranger* reveal the stance of those who use this language:

> one who is neither a friend nor an acquaintance
> a foreigner, a newcomer, or an outsider
> one who is unaccustomed to or unacquainted with something
> specific; a novice
> a visitor or guest

one that is neither privy nor party to a title, an act, or a contract[1]

Of these definitions, only the last can be used to describe the gay/lesbian Christian's status in the church, for the other definitions do not apply to those who have been baptized and have experienced their lives of faith in the Christian church. We are friends, acquaintances, insiders, and family members, accustomed to the traditions and rituals. We have sat on committees, paid our tithes, prayed for the sick, and fed the hungry. Once we cross over the "don't ask, don't tell" line, however, and speak of our total self, we are pushed out of the supposed bounds of Christianity. "No more of God's grace for you until you fix yourself," they seem to say.

Who is the actor? Whose actions create the stranger? Is it the gay or lesbian—perhaps a friend and family member—who makes herself or himself known and therefore is considered strange? Or is it the ruling members of the Christian community who deem us strange? Who takes children of God and labels them foreign?

From the same dictionary, definitions of the verb *estrange* prove helpful in discerning whose action creates the notion of a stranger:

> to make hostile, unsympathetic, or indifferent; alienate
> to remove from an accustomed place or set of associations
> to treat as a stranger, disown[2]

The actor is the Church when its leaders tell gay and lesbian Christians that God does not find them acceptable. Christian brothers and sisters decide that homosexuals do not meet the standards that would allow them to associate with Christian people and share their identity as children of God. The Church deems us strange.

Biblical Images

What does the Bible tell us about strangers? Looking through the Old Testament, we find numerous references to strangers (sojourners, aliens).[3] Many command that hospitality be shown to the stranger, reminding the ancient reader of times when they also were estranged. "You shall not wrong or oppress a resident alien (stranger), for you were aliens in the land of Egypt" (Exod. 22:21). (See also Deut. 10:18, 19; 26:11; Ps. 146:9.)

Other verses describe the practice of strangers having similar obligations to obey the law. "But the seventh day is a Sabbath to the LORD your God; in it you shall not do any work—you, your son or daughter, your male or female slave, your livestock, or the alien resident in your towns" (Exod. 20:10). (See also Exod. 12:19 and Num. 15:30.)

Strangers in Israel were resident aliens, with certain conceded but not inherited political rights.[4] Scriptures continuously directed Israel to include the stranger, which served as constant reminders that the resident stranger was still an alien with no familial protection.

Strangers were made members of the community by the laws of hospitality, not because they were born into the family. In contrast, baptized gay/lesbian persons are made members of the community because we are born into the family of God through God's mark upon us, not because the church has obeyed the laws of hospitality.

As we search the New Testament, there is a compelling argument for rejecting the identity of stranger and embracing the identity of family/friends.

> But now in Christ Jesus you who once were far off have been brought near by the blood of Christ. . . . So then you are no longer strangers and aliens, but you are citizens with the saints and also members of the household of God, built upon the foundation of the apostles and prophets, with Christ Jesus himself as the cornerstone. In him the whole structure is joined together and grows into a holy temple in the Lord; in whom you also are built together spiritually into a dwelling place for God.
>
> (Eph. 2:13–22)

How does the church today communicate who is included and who is not—who is citizen and who is alien? Today, the church does not talk of inherited rights. The church talks of faith, except when it talks of gays and lesbians. The church claims that homosexuals exclude themselves by "immoral" acts; not even faith can overcome works. Our Christian identity is reduced to our sexual orientation, which in turn is reduced solely to our acts of sexual intercourse.

Is the Church being honest about the roots of judgment? Are the roots established in God's love, or steeped in cultural norms that breed fear and hostility? If indeed lesbian and gay Christians are the stranger outside of the family of God, unchosen people, it seems that the Bible teaches the church to include them—even further, for the church not to oppress them. "Let mutual love continue. Do not neglect to show hospitality to strangers, for by doing that some have entertained angels without knowing it" (Heb. 13:1, 2).

If we are the stranger, then we can expect hospitality from the people of God. However, hospitality and self-righteousness have been flip-flopped. The lesbian and gay stranger is accused of the sin of Sodom when the sin of Sodom was actually the refusal to show hospitality to the strange angels present in the city (Gen. 19:1–29). Bruce Hilton argues:

> It is more likely that the fatal sin of Sodom was violation of the sacred trust of hospitality the Hebrew people were supposed to show to strangers. There are many other passages in the Bible that mention Sodom, and the sins that all but the most recent two denounce are selfishness, arrogance, and inhospitality.
> (See Isa. 1, Jer. 23, and Jesus' words in Luke 10:10–12.)[5]

It may be splitting hairs to distinguish between misnaming children of God as the stranger and violating the stranger, for both are oppressive acts stemming from the same source: fear of "the other." When we understand the other as a reflection of ourselves, we recognize the power of self-fear. Few want to be the outsider, the stranger; but, instead of including all, we begin to draw circles around ourselves which exclude the "other" and secure ourselves.

The Church's Investment in the Stranger

◆ *Barriers of Fear*

The Church often places barriers between non-gays/lesbians and gays/lesbians who would ordinarily participate together in the life of the Church. Consider one journalist's portrayal of anti-gay/lesbian rhetoric:

> *Stranger! Stranger! You are so strange! You are so strange that you cannot be part of God! So strange that you cannot be human! You are so strange that that is the only reason that Christians would think to love you!*
>
> Of course, that's it! The fear of self, the fear of the same gender, one like us must be made STRANGE, must be made distant, cannot be seen as like me, for then others might think that I am strange. The circle spins and spins and spins and spins until the whole world is dizzy with spinning in lies and deceit and judgment, until the whole word finds little

> room for loving and accepting and caring. *Stranger means no*
> *obligation, no civil rights accorded, their blood must be spilled,*
> *their tainted blood of Satan.*[6]

To this I respond:

> My God, my God, why has thou forsaken me? How long, O
> Lord will we cry out to you? How long, O Lord . . .[7]

Why the fear of gay and lesbian people? Why the investment in
stereotypes and general statements about the power of homosexuals
to destroy the very fabric of American society? Fear separates. Labels
differentiate. Categories distance. But why? Where is one's faith?

Our culture's faith is in the traditional family: dad, mom, son-billy,
and daughter-susie. Our culture's tradition is to hide emotion, seek
after the Ameri-suburbia Dream; don't question happiness; don't
question the story line; just live it; it will make you happy. And don't
forget to put the roast in the oven before you go to church on Sunday.

Clearly, the lives of gay/lesbian Christians question the traditional
standard. "These people are not living out the script; they have the
audacity to reject it, and actually pursue their own lives," society
seems to say. "They must be stopped."

The Church's trust is in conventional structures, not in a God who
is creating anew, making a way in the wilderness. The Church's faith
is in maintaining customs rather than seeking justice. To open up
and embrace homosexuality is to go against the cultural tide.

It is difficult to go against such a force; it questions some very basic tenets that we have been taught since the cradle. To shift one of
the basic foundations of our societal life is to leave us free-falling, not
knowing where we will land or what will be left to hold us up.

Rather than question deep-seated gender roles that have been the
bedrock for patriarchal social structures, the church labels chal-
lengers to the system as strangers. Just how pervasive are these social patterns? Carter Heyward writes:

> In a society, essentially a contemporary world order, built
> upon sex roles; an economy—namely capitalism (although
> Marxism has a similar set of sex-role problems)—maintained
> upon sex roles; a religion—Christianity—thoroughly patriar-
> chal and rooted in sex roles, the deepest currents of women's
> liberation and gay/lesbian liberation merge in radical femi-
> nism and threaten to bring down the entire social/eco-
> nomic/religious structure of reality.

Many fear that lesbian feminism poses a threat to the nuclear family, the economic order, the religious assumptions about marriage as the blessed state, the fatherhood of God and the motherhood of women, the procreative norm of sexuality, and the high value of dominant-submissive relationships beginning with male property rights and extending to God the Father. Those who fear that this is what we are about fear rightly. As lesbian, feminist, Christian, I believe that our vocation is to bring down the sacred canopy that has heretofore prevented our active realization of love and justice in human life as the only sacred—godly, right, and normative—dimension of our life together on earth.[8]

Naturally there is resistance; however, it is *unexamined* resistance that is dangerous. To make the blanket statement that homosexuals are the problem is to avoid looking at the log in one's own heterosexual eye. It denies that the culturally preferred relational structures are often unjust and destructive.

The fact that so many women die at the hands of their husbands is abysmal.[9] The number of children who are victims of incest in traditional families is heinous. If generalizations were to count for something, every pastor who does preheterosexual-marriage counseling should have a serious talk with the woman about the real danger that is present. If the most appalling behavior of some heterosexual men was considered the norm, then women who date men would have to be warned of the heterosexual male's propensity to look at women as property—property to be stalked and murdered if the woman ever leaves the man.

Though the statistics tell us of the violence in a woman's world, especially the violence perpetrated by men she knows, the culture does not make negative stereotypes about heterosexuality. Hetero-affection is not reduced to the exceptions as homo-affection is. Again, the mythical traditional family is set up as the ideal. As Suzanne Pharr writes:

Heterosexism is the systematic display of homophobia in the institutions of society. Heterosexism and homophobia work together to enforce compulsory heterosexuality and that bastion of patriarchal power, the nuclear family. The central focus of the right wing attack against women's liberation is that women's equality, women's self-determination, women's control of our own bodies and lives will damage what they see as the crucial societal institution, the nuclear family. . . .

their [right wing] passion has led them to bomb women's clinics and to recommend deprogramming for homosexuals and establishing camps to quarantine people with AIDS. To resist marriage and/or heterosexuality is to risk severe punishment and loss.[10]

Against the backdrop of the rhetoric of the religious right, the moderate-to-liberal mainline churches' silence and complacency towards gays/lesbians serves as a conspiratory green light to those who would do us violence. The religious right has bought enough television and radio time to be the loudspeaker behind all of society. Lesbian and gay people are their newest target on which to project fear and disgust, manipulating dollars out of the pockets of those who believe their fear tactics. While the elevator music of hatred is being heard openly or subliminally by millions of people, the general public hears few Christian leaders stand against these messages of hatred and self-righteousness.

What is at stake here? First, precious lives are. Second, the gospel of love is at stake. Finally, the conscious effort of mainline churches to recapture the prophetic voice of the One who leads them is at stake. Where is our calling—to love or to hate? To fear or to understand? Of which is the church an instrument?

The prophetic lives and loves of lesbian and gay families witness to a faith that is not enmeshed in societal norms but empowered in the God who sets us free. This is not a stranger's faith. Gary David Comstock reflects:

> If we are ever pressed to name a role model for ourselves from scripture, I think we have found one in Queen Vashti. Vashti seems simply to have preferred to stay with the women at the banquet she was giving for them and to have had the good sense and self-esteem to refuse to appear before the drunken emperor as a sexual object for display. But Vashti's decision, grounded in good sense, dignity, or independence, threatened the empire's social order (Esther 1).
>
> We are not unlike Vashti, and her story is not unlike ours. As lesbians and gay men, we have decided to restore and establish something as basic as our affectional preference, our dignity, our right to love; and something as simple as our act to decide, think, and feel for ourselves has made the church nervous to the point of fearing that our living our lives as fully human beings threatens the foundations of family structure, the natural order, and traditional social relations. . . .

While it may not have been our intention, I think we have to face squarely that our very lives, when lived openly and fully, fundamentally threaten the social order. When we begin to make decisions for ourselves instead of letting others tell us how we should live, we challenge those who have power at the expense of the disempowered and marginalized.[11]

What if we dreamed of a different world? What if we allowed our minds to wander on the frontier of relationships, imagining the ideal of ideals? Would we need to be so specific about gender and gender roles? What if our minds were free to imagine that our greatest desires for primary relationships could be met? What would that experience be? What would it feel, smell, taste like? Is it possible that God the creator of love would want this for us? *Yes*.

◆ Barrier to Sexuality

Another barrier that the Church erects is between sexuality and spirituality. The resulting schism divides our whole selves and wreaks havoc on many. One young lesbian writes:

> not having any talk about sex in my family made it very difficult once i got married. it wasn't that we were told not to talk about it. it was just that there was such a silence on it. no talks about menstruation or dating or sexuality at all. i had no one to talk to. i did not know that other people were open about it. i thought that i was all alone in my misery. the first time i went to a Gyn was 6 weeks before my wedding. the doctor was condescending, telling me that birth control pills had no side effects and that my concerns were unfounded. don't ask, don't talk about it was his message. and once i was married and had pain with sex, had discomfort rather than passion, who could i go to? who could i talk to? finally i got an infection so bad with soreness and pain so bad that i had a reason to ask timidly among some female acquaintances what doctor they would recommend . . . later in my marriage when we would have terrible fights about me not wanting to have sex, i felt so isolated, i felt like things were never going to change, i was not going to change, i felt so alone, i just wanted to end my life, i felt like a failure to god and to myself, that i could not be the godly wife. i thought that there was no escape except death . . . would it have helped if i

hadn't been taught that sex before marriage was sinful? would i have been better off being able to explore my sexuality before marriage? as a lesbian, i think so. because i thought the good wife tapes would just kick in. sex had been so romanticized and sensationalized that i thought the magic would just happen ... but then, and only then, did i first know that heterosexuality was not for me. the pain of that realization once the "i will's" were said . . . the "death do us part" was spoken . . . how alone i felt without one person with whom to share my fears and failures. . . .

From a lesbian woman, name withheld

Part of the complexity of accepting homosexuality is the struggle to fully embrace sexuality in general. Early on in Christianity, sexuality was split off from spirituality, the flesh from the spirit. As Augustine argued that sexuality is the source of sin rather than a dimension of "sacred passion," he set in motion a "violent antagonism" that we suffer from to this day. It is astounding to think that for 1600 years the connection between God and sex has been broken and denied.[12]

The consequences of this split, this breaking off of sexuality as sinful, are devastating to gay and non-gay alike. Having a core part of ourselves that we are taught to tightly fear, question, and control, creates a society that is out of touch with a primal force. What we fear most is what controls us. We are a culture where sex is the elusive god; sex sells; sex objectifies; sex satisfies. We are so wonderfully made! Yet we are told in church that part of our very selves is sinful. In order to be spiritual, we must deny our bodily needs; and, most especially, deny our sexual needs.

What results from centuries of disconnecting sexuality from spirituality, making the former negative and the latter positive? What happens when the spirit is taken out of the body? Today we reap the results of having sown a disembodied faith. As exemplified in pornography, we have displaced "sensual, mutual relationships by objectifying fantasy." Many are more excited by watching than by actual loving and sensuous intercourse.[13]

We of the incarnational faith—Emmanuel, God with us—have pushed away our bodily integrity. We struggle with accepting our sexuality as a gift from God intended to enliven and nurture us, to bond and connect us. The gift has been ignored for so long that the gift has become the means of dominance, terror, advertising, exploitation, and spiritual death. As James Nelson suggests:

The sixth deadly sin of which our religious traditions are often guilty is a sexless image of spirituality. . . . In its more extreme forms, such a view perceived true spirituality as sexless, celibacy as meritorious, and bodily mortification and pain as conducive to spiritual purification.[14]

The fear and repression of sexuality in general fan the flames of homophobia. If one is not to value one's bodily existence but to somehow fear or downplay it, how does one respond to questions about sexuality at all? With great resistance, I suspect. The inner tug is to avoid, deplore, and deny. The walls go up, the sentry is on the lookout.

In order to move anywhere with discussions about sexual orientation, the church family must be willing to face the fear of sexuality in general. James B. Nelson writes of his own experience,

> One thing that I discovered was that homophobia was a particularly acute problem for males—it certainly was for me. For the first time I realized that my fear of lesbians and gays was connected to issues in my own masculine identity. Gay males seemed to have an ill-defined masculinity, a threat to any man in a society where one's masculinity seems never achieved once and for all and always needs proving. Lesbians threatened my masculinity simply because they were living proof that at least some women did not need a man to validate or complete them as persons. . . .
>
> Further, confronting my own fears meant confronting my fears of sexuality as such—my erotophobia. Though I had long enjoyed the sexual experience, I came to realize that, reared in a dualistic culture, I was more distanced from my sexuality than I cared to admit. Reared as a male and conditioned to repress most bodily feelings, reared as "a good soldier" and taught to armor myself against any emotional or physical vulnerability, I discovered I was more alienated from my body than I had acknowledged. Gay males and lesbians brought into some kind of dim awareness my own erotophobia because they represented sexuality in a fuller way.[15]

Chapter 2 carefully detailed the manifestations of silence; the Church needs to examine the consequences of this spiritual isolation. We must affirm that our sexual selves cannot be separated from our spiritual selves. No matter what, our sexual/spiritual cries will be heard. Consider David Crawford's words:

But in fact the most furtive aspect of compulsive anonymous sex often isn't the sex itself—it's the silent, blind, tender gesture. This is the soul reaching out. And the soul will reach out, no matter if you're in a men's room stall or an orgy room of a back-room bar. We know this, deeply—we all know this—but we hide it as if it were the most terrible, inadmissible secret of all.[16]

When the Church brings sexuality and spirituality together, it can return to an embodied faith. When church family members integrate their lives and cease fearing their sexual selves, the church will come closer to all of creation. The Church will cease estrangement and move toward embodiment.

◆ Barriers to Relationships

Prescribed gender roles and expectations are yet another barrier the Church constructs, leaving gays/lesbians as well as non-gays/lesbians stifled. Consider one lesbian's despair:

the church did not tell me what to do when i didn't like men, when i didn't care to flirt or give my power over to men, all they told me then was that i was just selfish and obstinate and against God's will . . . i must be broken . . . and, i was, as i married and prayed desperately each day to be a good wife . . . each day . . . not to enjoy life, not to understand myself, not to question my sadness, or to strengthen my relationship, but how to fill a role that would be worthy of God's approval . . . how i ached because the love did not come, the obedience was not there, and then when this husband told me that my body was not my own, that he owned it, that he could touch me if he wanted, that i should want to have sex with him— even when it was painful, even when i was repulsed, even then because that's what it meant to be a good wife . . . and i felt strange and lonely, and sad and helpless and hopeless, trapped, lost, sinking deeper with each prayer to make me submissive. . . .

From a lesbian woman, name withheld

Unexamined fear feeds unexamined power, and so it goes with homophobia. As noted in chapter 2, Suzanne Pharr defines homophobia as "the irrational fear and hatred of those who love and sexually desire those of the same sex."[17] Homophobia often goes unexamined because the darkness of fear is many times projected onto homosexuals, accusing us of being the problem rather than the problem being the irrational fear.

Fear distances and separates. Fear legislates against relating to one another: "We won't have lesbians living next door to us." Fear says, "We won't have gays in our churches, it would scare away the families with young children." "If my child told me that he was gay, I would disown him." "Gays and lesbians cannot be in the military because they threaten national security." "Beware of strangers."

When fear and legislation (institutional power) go hand in hand, homophobia has moved beyond an irrational fear to become the irrational control/judgment of fellow children of God. Homophobia moves into the realm of what Christine Smith calls "radical evil," it becomes part of the interlocking system of oppression.[18] Smith elaborates:

> There is a kind of righteous judgment that flows from the pulpits of this land that ought to be of major concern for every thinking, sensitive person. In the name of the Christian gospel the everyday lives and rights of gay and lesbian persons are actively violated. . . . Through its theologies, biblical interpretations, and sexual ethics, the Christian church is one of the primary institutions that provide a foundation for social and ecclesiastical oppression of lesbians and gay men.[19]

Searing-hot lava spewing from a volcano burns and destroys as it rushes down the mountain, leaving behind a scarred land. So it is with homophobia, except the land is a people, children of God, and the lava is a collection of choices made by others who refuse to question their fear, as Suzanne Pharr experienced.

> In my life I have experienced the effects of homophobia through rejection by friends, threats of loss of employment, and threats upon my life; and I have witnessed far worse things happening to other lesbian and gay people: loss of children, beatings, rape, death. Its power is great enough to keep ten to twenty percent of the population living lives of fear (if their sexual identity is hidden) or lives of danger (if their sexual identity is visible) or both. And its power is great enough to keep the remaining eighty to ninety percent of the population trapped in their own fears. . . . What is unhealthy—and sometimes a source of stress and sickness so great it can lead to suicide—is homophobia, that societal

disease that places such negative messages, condemnation, and violence on gay men and lesbians that we have to struggle throughout our lives for self-esteem.[20]

Homophobia poisons everyone, gay and non-gay, as it seeps into our unwritten rules of relating to each other. Men are to be men; women are to be women. Men can have men-friends but not too intimate friends. Women can have close women-friends but these relationships are swiftly relegated or cut off when a woman's man comes home. Men can shower together but not share the same bed; women can share a double bed but can't expose themselves in the nakedness of a shower stall. Men must exude machismo or they will be called "fairies." Women are to be dependent on men, passive not aggressive, or they will be called "dykes." Homophobia burns reality, stunts growth, and tries to force our self-identities into small molds of gender-being.

Paul's writings in 1 Corinthians also reflect heterosexist role-keeping. Violating the rigidly prescribed power roles of men and women was the abomination: for a man to be in a passive role during sex was to act like a woman and degrade his manly nature, for a woman to assume the dominant role was equally unnatural.[21]

Pharr writes of the three weapons used to keep women in their place: economics, violence, and homophobia.[22] These weapons cause or threaten women with pain or loss. In battering relationships, women are controlled by violence and threats of violence so that they fear for their lives and the lives of their children and doubt the realities of their own abilities and self-value. They are beaten because they are not measuring up or for not being passive. They are beaten for being lesbian or because they stood up for themselves as no "real woman" would. And the male batterer often feels justified, even righteous, for his part in keeping women in their place.[23]

Audre Lorde relayed similar thoughts within her essay "Scratching the Surface."[24] She goes a step further, though, in describing what threats of abandonment do to women's friendship and solidarity:

> All too often the message comes loud and clear to Black women from Black men: "I am the only prize worth having and there are not too many of me, and remember, I can always go elsewhere. So if you want me, you'd better stay in your place which is away from one another, or I will call you a 'lesbian' and wipe you out." Black women are programmed to define ourselves within this male attention and to compete

with each other for it rather than to recognize and move
upon our common interests.[25]

Pharr names the force and threat behind calling a woman a lesbian as "lesbian baiting . . . an attempt to control women by labeling
us as lesbians because our behavior is not acceptable" as when "we
resist male dominance and control. And it has little or nothing to do
with one's sexual identity."[26]

"Lesbian baiting" or "fag baiting" keeps the limits drawn. Who is
in and who is not; who is familiar, who is "stranger." The church in-
vests in the stranger image and thus in homophobia and heterosexism to maintain the status quo, to keep women in a subservient role
and men in a dominant one. The supposed benefits are order, clarity, and love of God and country. But how can we talk of love while
it is denied within gender groups? What and who are the casualties
of the church's investment in homophobia and heterosexism?

What happens to the way that women relate to each other if they
fear being called a lesbian, if there is the threat of rejection and violence? What happens when two men approach deeper intimacy?
What fears end up destroying the magnificence of interpersonal
bonding? Life is cut off before it reaches the cusp. Gifts of love and
happiness are scarred by societal fears; the apex of friendship is not
reached but denied. What happens to a society that fails to fully experience intimacy, compassion, and empathy?

The casualty list goes something like this:

> roles, not relationships;
> disembodied sexuality and spirituality;
> alienation, isolation, low self-esteem, depression;
> anger, resentment, hatred;
> despondency, destructive behaviors, suicide;
> breakdown of empathy, community, connectedness.

All of these are sacrificed, in the name of righteousness.

In view of the destructive and often passive role the church plays
in the lives of gay/lesbian Christians, the Church must be confronted
with its ethical responsibility to shape the self-identity of gays/les-
bians as children of God. With Archbishop Tutu, may the Church
recognize, "Oppression is not only evil, it is blasphemous because it
makes a child of God doubt that s/he is a child of God."[27]

The Church as family needs to be held accountable to the baptismal covenant into which it entered and continues to enter with

each child of God. Chapter 4 will further discuss the implications of sacramental theology, and in chapter 5 we will return to the opportunities that await the Church in remembering and being thankful for its lesbian sisters and gay brothers.

To the people of courage who cannot live within the societal molds, there is the threat of rejection and danger. For lesbian and gay people, rejection and danger are risked for the greater worth of loving and accepting oneself, for the beauty of relationships born of honesty and truth, and for the very essence of being ourselves. Courage transcends fear to find understanding and relationship. The "stranger" label is cast off; the children of God rejoice; the Church embodies the freedom of the gospel.

ELAINE

How many times did I feel like an outsider? How many times did I feel someone staring coldly at me because I was different and did not belong? I know now that although these reoccurring feelings appeared to create obstacles in my early search for faith as a child, I want to describe how I eventually found an image of God with which I can now identify.

Emotional security and confidence were not traits I related to very easily, even though I was surrounded by the love and a secure home provided by my loving and financially fit family. I grew up in the prominent Park Cities near Dallas, an area where the average income level seemed to hold more value than anything else. Seeking success was a daily occurrence; my brother and I were taught and encouraged through a superior private-school type education, and supported by savvy-minded parents who dreamt of us creating a future much brighter than their own.

I enjoyed the prosperous surroundings and know now that the environment I knew so well built an important stepping stone for seeking uniqueness and finding value in my own spiritual discipline.

The very large, very heterosexual Presbyterian church I loved so dearly meant no harm. I only knew that there were days when I did not feel loved for my differences and found myself questioning whether I was loved by anyone, especially my God. I remember hearing a sermon when I was about thirteen or fourteen years old, where the pastor mentioned that "there may even be one homosexual in our congregation!" The message I remember was that we ought to encourage anyone who may be different from "us" to stay in the church anyway, that at least this homosexual's children might have a chance for re-demption and healing. What I heard was that accepting my own sex-uality was wrong—a sin—and that anyone with these feelings needs to abandon them, redeem themselves and recover. Was homosexual-ity an illness? I felt perfectly well!

This sermon, of course, made me very angry, for at that age, I was beginning to realize that my own sexuality truly existed with over-whelming power, and that I have a genuine love for other women. I knew this because, since I was at least seven years old, I always had special feelings for the girls in my classes and the female influences in my life, and it felt fine and natural. So after thinking about that sermon, I felt very rejected. Now I know why, for so many years, I had not felt encouraged or supported to be the me I knew so well.

And so shortly after high school, I began my search for a place where I fit. I found a Bible church in the same neighborhood as my previous church that was not afraid to mention the word "homosex-ual," and I learned that a support group of gay men met weekly at the church. Could this be a place for me? Well, I later discovered, to my surprise, that these men had agreed to vows of celibacy! Again, only partial acceptance—but even greater denial pushed me to keep on searching.

At many churches I visited, I felt pushed into the singles category. The assumption was, and still seems today, that any female between nineteen and thirty-five must primarily seek a male mate before the rest of God's plan would take course. This constant categorizing got very old, as matrimony simply was not the focus of my own spiritual search. Can't churches find other ways to group us?

I ventured to the Oak Lawn area and to my happy relief found a place where God was not known as condemning, but as loving and nurturing, and accepting of the kind of love I knew so well in my heart. I discovered that at least ten churches in the Dallas area have a gay and lesbian outreach, and for that I am truly grateful. At one particular church, I found the focus of many discussions on the idea of "inclusive language." What a new idea, that there are many more understandings and interpretations of God's word and God's perception than that of a white, blue-eyed blond male. It seems to me and many who work hard to reeducate and rejuvenate our religious language that there must be as many visions of God as there are people on this earth. For example, if I had grown up Asian-Indian, wouldn't I perceive God as having my own color and speaking my own language? Also, we understand God as the Father, but isn't God also portrayed as the Mother? If I had grown up in a family with an abusive father, I may never choose to see God simply because I may be afraid of men. But now we understand that God has many facets and many faces, and that we may re-image our God of understanding to one of a loving power who indeed loves us back. By accepting inclusivity in our language, it is possible to accept diversity and accept that our differences and uniqueness no longer need be compromised. What an incredible opportunity for greater love in our world!

After a short time, Metropolitan Community Church became my church home. Over the weeks and months, I found myself craving for the fellowship of this loving congregation. Before this period in my life, I had not fully understood the value of the commitment to a church family and its community. I knew it now. Not only did I attend weekly worship, but I found myself becoming more active as a volunteer, first as an usher (women didn't get to usher at my old church!) and later assisting the development of discipleship classes for new members. I know now that God has my hand and I am happy to follow in the journey!

Each week at worship service we take Communion. I had only experienced a weekly breaking of bread when I was dating a Catholic woman a few years earlier. Now I understand the value of sharing the meal and accepting the blood and body of the spirit. There are many times when I recall my own acceptance of Jesus Christ in my life. I knew it as a teenager, and again felt renewed during my process of joining the Metropolitan Community Church. Before Confirmation Sunday, I had a long talk with a lesbian friend who had attended seminary for many years, and I decided that I would be re-baptized at this time. I knew that the abundance and beauty of water in our world represents the constant flow of the Holy Spirit in our lives, and because of that incredible and precious love I felt and experienced, I chose to again accept the sacrament of Baptism. Like myself, so many receive baptism shortly after birth, at the decision of their parents. I now knew that since I had found my new family, it was extremely important to consciously accept Christ into my life again, in a fuller and more whole way than I had known before. So with joy in my heart and tears in my eyes, I joined the Metropolitan Community Church on Palm Sunday, 1990.

As an adult, I have a new willingness to accept a spiritual life on a level that is more truly representative of an all-encompassing love. Although sometimes I felt limited during my first twenty years of religious experience, I now see that time as merely a part of the process of seek-

ing spiritual guidance. And through a process of cleansing and re-
newal, I also found greater personal and public acceptance of my own
sexuality, and later, the courage to come out to my own parents and
brother.

I know that I could have told them much sooner, as I had been out
for almost ten years by this point. But somehow it was crucial that I
build a support system of love and understanding before divulging the
news that I had kept to myself for so long. I befriended several people
who had experienced coming out to their parents. I talked with the parents of a few other gays and lesbians. I discussed at length the questions and concerns that might have come up, and I prepared myself,
over the course of a year, to break the news to my mom, dad, and
brother. As a result, I was able to handle the questions, concerns, and
fears with greater strength and understanding—with the help of God
and some dear friends close by my side.

I sense that, beginning when we are very young, we may tend to
limit our own beliefs and acceptance levels in much the same way that
our parents meant well by leading and protecting and encouraging (or
discouraging) us as best they could, based on their understanding of
our situations.

I know now that God shows me the power of choice. I also realize
the importance of empowering our inner selves through questions and
soul-searching journeys—if only we accept them and enjoy the ride!

MATTHEW

"I like men," he said. "I've always been more attracted to men than
to women, both physically and emotionally. What I'm saying is that
I'm gay." It was late September, and I had met this man soon after I began my first year of seminary. His words left me in shock, and I had no
idea how to respond to him. I was literally left speechless.

I thanked him for sharing his story with me, but underneath that su-
perficial response, a mixture of emotion was building inside of me.
This person had put into words things I had been feeling for many
years. Even though I didn't know it that night, his willingness to risk
coming out to me would have a profound impact on me and would
change not only my understanding of myself but also my understanding of the Church.

I was the third and last child in my family. My parents and my older
brother and sister had always been involved in a local suburban
United Methodist Church, so soon after my birth, I was baptized into

God's family. Of course, since my baptism occurred when I was an infant, I don't remember any of the details. I have been told about that day, including who was there and what happened and the name of the minister who dripped water on my head. All I know for sure is that I never questioned my baptism. Knowing that I was a child of God was very important to me as I grew up and became involved in the church.

The one thing I remember very vividly about my youth was the time I spent at church. It was like a second home to me. As a young child, I always went with my family to Sunday services and Sunday school, and I attended vacation Bible school. I became even more involved as I got older, and following the traditional model, I was confirmed during the seventh grade. I went to confirmation classes for several Sundays before the pastor laid his hands on me during one late-Sunday-morning service and proclaimed me a full member of the Church. Finally, I was no longer a probationary member! I was a full member of my church, and I took that commitment very seriously. I pledged one-tenth of my allowance. I kept perfect attendance in Sunday school. I sang in the youth choir and played in the bell choir. I was a Boy Scout in the troop that met at the church. I was active in Bible studies. I was a member of the Youth Fellowship and was elected president. I went on a summer work-camp trip. I was involved in clown ministry. Church was truly my second home, and there were some weeks when I spent more time at church than I did at my own home.

A few folks tried to persuade me that I should think about ministry as a vocation. Ignoring their nudging, I went off to college to major in computer science. College life was much the same for me as I became involved in a church close to campus and sometimes attended Sunday school or Bible studies. I went on retreats and was involved in Bible studies in my residence hall. I continued, on a limited basis, to put on a mask of white greasepaint and a costume to participate in clown ministry, and I worked on a church-camp staff for a summer. I still had people nudging me to think about going into full-time ministry.

During these high school and college years, when it came to dating, relationships, and sexuality, I was one of the most naive persons around. I dated very little—only twice during high school and college. I wasn't interested in girls and took my fair share of teasing because of it. However, I did find guys to be the subject of both my interest and my fantasy. I didn't understand why I wasn't attracted to girls like other guys I knew, so I always shrugged it off as "a stage" I was going through. I believed I would eventually grow out of it. When folks asked if there was someone special, I usually said that I wasn't interested in dating a lot, but instead was waiting for the right girl to come along. And that's what I believed. The word *homosexuality* was not a part of my vocabulary, and it was not something that was discussed among my friends or my family, or in school or in church—or anywhere, at least that I can remember. All the feelings I had about other guys were kept deep inside of me, and guilt and shame were the result of those feelings. I would fantasize about other guys and later ask God's forgiveness and help in changing me.

It was during my junior year in college that I decided computer science wasn't what I wanted to do with my life. So I started listening to all the folks who had thought I should go to seminary. An interesting thing began to happen: when I told people that I was thinking about becoming an ordained minister in the United Methodist Church, no one seemed surprised. My friends and family were all very, very supportive. This only confirmed what I understood as my call to ministry and gave me confidence to move ahead. I was soon certified as a candidate for ordained ministry and headed off to study in Dallas, Texas. The only thing troubling me about this decision was the lingering attractions I still had—attractions that I believed were something other than normal. Those attractions had only become stronger, and I constantly wondered how I could be called to ministry and still be experiencing these things. Nevertheless, I believed that if God was calling me to ministry, then God would also take care of these things that were tearing at my insides. I would soon be surprised at how God would take care of these things.

It was during September of my first semester of seminary that my friend and fellow seminary student came out to me. My reaction to him was emotional chaos. I was excited because someone I had grown to respect had finally put into words all the things I had felt for so many years. For the first time in my life, I knew that I was not alone. I was not the only one to have experienced things that I thought were other than normal and about which I could not and must not talk. Finally, I began the process of accepting those feelings and attractions as good. But I was also scared to death, because if I decided to tell him, he would be the only person to know my deep, dark secrets. They would no longer be buried inside for only me to see. Did I want to tell someone that I was attracted to other men? For so long I had felt this was a phase I would grow out of. Now I was beginning to accept that I might be gay and that it might be okay to be gay. That was a very frightening change for me.

I did come out to myself—and to that friend. He also became my first lover. Over the next few months, with his help, I began to become comfortable with being gay. It was really very easy because it felt so natural and right and normal for me. It was a great release of a lot of years of feelings and emotions, but it raised many questions too, especially since I was a seminary student. I began to read everything I could get my hands on, and I also began to struggle with reconciling my gay identity with my call to ordained ministry. That process has never ended, since most churches do not believe that those persons who are gay or lesbian can also be called to ministry.

During the first few months after my coming out, I easily became comfortable with being gay, and I learned a lot about being gay. I learned about what the Church has traditionally said about homosexuality, and I learned about the changes in the medical and psychological fields regarding sexuality in general. I found out what it's like to have my roommate walk in on my lover and me in an intimate embrace—and the next day to feel like I was walking around campus with a sign around my neck saying, "I'm gay."

My first relationship ended the next spring, but I continued to read and study and learn about what being gay was going to mean for me. Since I was no longer "attached," I began to struggle with one big question, "Do I need to be in a relationship (which for me also meant not being closeted) or can I be celibate (and thus remain in the closet)?" If I could be celibate and closeted, then continuing toward the goal of ordination would not be a problem. However, if I needed and wanted to be in a relationship, then being ordained would be a bit more of a problem. As I thought more about this question, I became more and more angry at the Church for putting gays and lesbians in a spot where there has to be a choice. The fact is, no matter which I chose—to be closeted and ordained, or to be open and not ordained—I would lose something very important. This is the anger I have felt ever since: that the Church would force gays to choose between being openly and honestly who we are and being ordained.

As for me, I chose the first. I decided that for me, being in a relationship and not having to be closeted were more important than having the Church's blessing on my ministry. I did finish my seminary degree, including a full year of internship working as a chaplain in a hospital, and my second lover—life partner—and I have now been together for almost six years. But since my coming to terms with who I am as a gay man, I have retreated, sometimes slowly and sometimes quickly, from the church. I am a baptized Christian with a seminary degree, and yet the Church is the place where I feel the least at home.

Very rarely will you find me in church on a Sunday morning, or any other time, because church is the place where I cannot be myself. It is the place that was my second home growing up but is now the place I avoid like a plague. Now, instead of being an ordained minister and serving a church somewhere back where I grew up, I spend my time working in a clerical job for which I am overqualified. The question that I live with is what to do with a seminary degree if I am not serving in a church. And serving in a church would require me to suppress who I really am and thus to suppress the gifts I have for ministry.

The one place of refuge I have found is the Metropolitan Community Church (MCC) here in Dallas. It is a church with its primary ministry focused on gay and lesbian Christians. It is truly the only place in town that my partner and I can go and worship together. We can be ourselves there. The first time I attended the MCC, I cried through much of the service because I felt accepted there. For me, there is something very special about seeing a gay couple or a straight couple receiving Communion together—as a couple. And to be able to stand arm in arm with my partner as we sing a hymn together is the most liberating of moments. This would never happen in another church in Dallas.

Recently, the MCC held its Christmas Eve service at the Meyerson Symphony Center in downtown Dallas. The center holds somewhere around 2,500 people, and it was packed! As we sang the first hymn and I heard all my sisters' and brothers' voices, my heart filled with excitement. It had been a long time since I had felt the presence of God so strongly in a service of worship. As I reflect on that experience, I think about Holly Near's words, "We are a gentle, angry people, and we are singing, singing for our lives." We are a gentle people, and we are also an angry people because the church that proclaims Christ's love has failed to love us as we are, as baptized children of God. And we are singing because God has given us the gift of song so that we might sing out against all those who proclaim something other than God's love.

For me, the Church I grew up in and spent many hours in and loved and served has become my greatest oppressor. The Church says in many different ways that homosexuality is incompatible with Christianity, and yet in the love I share with my life partner, I experience God's love more fully than anywhere else. How can our love—indeed how can the love between any two people—be incompatible with anything?

I have never questioned my baptism. I have never questioned the fact that I am a child of God. I have never questioned the love God has for me. But I now question whether the church is really the Church! The church should be a gathering of the children of God who support and nurture and love one another and who celebrate and rejoice in God's unconditional love for all of God's creation. But the church has failed to show me these things because I am a gay man. It is my prayer that the church will hear itself singing the words of a great African-American spiritual: "We shall all be free . . . someday!" Someday is today, and now is the time for all of us to be free—free to love one another and to celebrate God's love for *all* of us.

4 ◆ Do This in Remembrance of Us

As many of you as were baptized into Christ have clothed yourselves with Christ. There is no longer Jew or Greek, there is no longer slave or free, there is no longer male and female, for all of you are one in Christ Jesus.

—Gal. 3:27–28

I assist with the baptism of an infant at the United Methodist Church I serve. The senior pastor calls the parents, the grandparents, the aunt, the uncle, and other sponsors forward to stand with this child. The child is at his best; he is smiling and cooing—taking in all of the colors and the lights around him. I watch him carefully as the questions are asked of his parents. Each question is read carefully, and each is answered with a firm "I do." The questions continue, and finally the crucial commitments are asked of the congregation. I look at this child and then peer out to the congregation as I speak, following the words of my church's hymnal:

> Do you, as Christ's body, the church, reaffirm both your rejection of sin and your commitment to Christ?

They answer loudly—"WE DO."

> Will you nurture one another in the Christian faith and life and include this child now before you in your care?

And they reply proudly,

> With God's help we will proclaim the good news
> and live according to the example of Christ.
> We will surround this child with a community of
> love and forgiveness, that he may grow in his
> service to others.
> We will pray for him
> that he may be a true disciple who walks in the way
> that leads to life.[1]

Then the baby is baptized with the water and the congregation rejoices with singing and smiles. Another creation of God, created in

69

the image of God, is marked as a child of Christ. As I watch the senior pastor take the baby into the congregation, I feel such sadness and think to myself:

> O little one, I wish I could say to you that we will keep that promise we have just spoken. I wish I could say that our love and acceptance will always be there for you no matter what your road. I wish I could even say this congregation will make every effort to love and support you—to raise you in the faith. I am sorry, for soon some of us will forget the covenant we have made. Others may remember occasionally. Fortunately, some people will remember always. Oh yes, little one, *one big warning:* If you step out of line . . . if you step out of the accepted boundaries of this church in order to be true to yourself and to the One who created you, the church will cut you off completely. We will turn against you. No questions asked. If you confess that you are a man who loves men, you will be ostracized, criticized, or at best, patronized. No longer will we remember the commitment we made at your baptism, whether you were a child or an adult. Some of us will become enraged with our own fear of you—the homosexual. Others will be indifferent and afraid to make waves or cause dissension. Your liberation will be no option whatsoever. Others will offer limited amounts or conditional offerings of support, and they will ride fences always. And you will find, little one, that the powerful words surrounding the covenant of your baptism will have fallen to the ground without much thought at all. But remember, God does remain faithful . . . God always remains faithful . . . even when human beings do not.

In reflection, I ask myself this question, "Is it not this same group of people who earlier, in the liturgy of the sacrament of Baptism, said that they rejected their sin?" Yet once the true identity of any gay/lesbian child of God is revealed, the church often makes the child believe that she or he is unworthy of God's grace and justice. Many of those same loving and supportive people now become sources of homophobia and prejudice, calling gay and lesbian Christians sinners, perverts, and even children of Satan. Have these people not broken the sacred covenant of grace and justice? Have they not forgotten to reject their sin and to reaffirm their commitment to Jesus the Christ? Could it be that the groups who place themselves on pedestals of holiness and self-righteousness are the ones who have insulted the sacrament of Baptism? Are they the ones who have committed an abomination?

In earlier chapters, we have tried with great effort to express the power of the sacraments in the overall issue of homosexuality. We have told the stories of gay and lesbian Christians who have received great pain and rejection from their churches. We have investigated how the Church silences homosexual persons and the effects that silencing has on them. We have explored the Church's use of the category stranger in an effort to be more benevolent. The Church now stands implicated in oppression. How can it, in good conscience, continue to marginalize any person, gay or straight, black or red, male or female, especially in the context of the sacraments? The sacraments alone call us to live a more faithful and just life—to be a people of a faith, which demands complete inclusiveness in the Church of Jesus Christ. The sacraments of Communion and Baptism are crucial actions within the Christian faith. To marginalize or reject any person is, in essence, an insult to the very purpose and theology of the sacraments. The questions are very clear: Do we as people of faith really mean what we say? Do we even do this in remembrance of Jesus?

The Sacraments As One Tapestry

In most mainline Protestant churches, the people of God celebrate two sacraments, Baptism and Holy Communion (The Lord's Supper). Protestant mainline churches believe that these two sacraments have been instituted by Christ as found in scripture, and that they are most definitely a means of grace. In essence, they actually convey God's grace. The sacraments are more than mere symbols or memorials to God. They are actively calling all of God's children to experience the grace of God. In the context of the sacraments, we as the body of Christ—the Church—celebrate Christ's presence and God's claim on us. The sacraments are vitally important because they call us to *remember* God's love and actions of liberation, to *experience* God's grace, and to *be* God's inclusive family.

Both Baptism and Communion are closely woven together, and their importance is vital to all Christians, especially those who are gay and lesbian. Sacramental theologian James White notes that Baptism is the sacrament that reflects the beginning of the Christian life, and Communion is the sacrament that sustains it. The two are different expressions of the unconditional, self-giving of God. Communion is the culminating act of Christian initiation, begun in the rite of Baptism; Communion is the only part of Baptism that is continually repeated.[2] In summary, Baptism marks us as children of God, and our taking of the bread and wine continually reaffirms that mark and our knowledge of it. Gay/Lesbian Christians often find their personal understanding of Baptism to be tainted and clouded by the homophobia of the Christian Church. It is very difficult to believe that we truly are marked and sealed as children of a loving and compassionate God. Once our view of Baptism has been distorted, then Communion also becomes confused. Homosexual Christians not only question their baptism but their real worthiness in the face of the sacrament of Communion. As gay/lesbian Christians question their vital role in the body of Christ and their worthiness for the sacraments, the experiences of Baptism and Communion are transformed from shouts and continual whispers of God's grace to continual screams of self-hatred and unworthiness.

Baptism and Its Importance

Most Christians have been baptized in one ritual form or another. They have been baptized as infants, as children, as youth, or as adults. Just as Jesus was baptized by John the Baptist (Matt. 3: 13–17), so too have we followed in the steps of Jesus and been baptized ourselves. Our baptism is vitally important to most of us, and often, we at least attempt to remember it and give thanks for it. At a summer camp several years ago, the camp design team agreed to do a "Service of Reaffirmation of the Baptismal Covenant."[3] Several on the team were very skeptical about the reactions of 250 junior-high youths to water being slung onto them by two well-meaning pastors. I must say that as I gathered around the large, plastic seashell overflowing with water that the youth had brought from home, I was uncertain about our decision. Yet the crowd fell silent as we blessed the water and explained our purpose. When we began to shout "Remember your baptism and be thankful!" and sling water across the group, I did not hear giggles and screams. Instead, I saw young men and women lean forward and lift their hands so that they might feel the water. They wanted to remember their baptism. They wanted to remember that first step in experiencing God's unconditional love and justice.

What is the meaning of this ritual of water in the Church of Jesus Christ? Why is it so important to the faith journey of every Christian? Baptism is the primary initiation act within the body of Christ. It is not the act of humanity, but the act of God. It is not earned, paid for, or sought after. Baptism is a pure gift that no one deserves but all can receive. We receive in the act of baptism.[4] Yet, this cannot be a passive receiving, as Marjorie Procter-Smith argues.

> Such a view of [passive] baptism leaves no room for the radical social equality expressed in the Galatians baptismal formula and intuited by Christian feminists, nor does it grant as baptismal birthright the necessity of engaging in continual struggle to bring the church and the world into harmony with the baptismal vision of equality.[5]

Baptism is most certainly a means of grace in which a person is called into the Church of Jesus Christ by the cleansing action of the water. The water signifies the liberating action of God[6] and unites the community of faith, bringing us together as one body. Baptism is a sacrament of equality that not only conveys or proclaims God's grace but also God's desire for justice and God's hope found in the reign of the Creator. Baptism becomes the foundation for justice within the Church because it is an impartial gift, an act of equality among all people. "We have all passed through the same waters and risen in the same body."[7] Baptism constantly calls us to remember the necessity for justice within the Church. "Every time we share in baptizing a new member into the body of Christ, we hear proclaimed the equality of all persons in the sight of God. Their full human worth is acted out in the water."[8] James White recognizes that we are no longer lost in an exclusive world, but ideally, are members of an inclusive body, the Church guided by its liberator, the Christ. As he writes here:

> there is an equality that Paul repeatedly ties to baptism. "There is no such thing as Jew and Greek, slave and freeman, male and female; for you are all one person in Christ Jesus" (Gal. 3:28) . . . our concern is to recognize our equality as recipients . . . God's self-giving is given indiscriminately to all those baptized, regardless of human differences. When we are brought to a place where there is water and submit to baptism, human distinctions disappear, and we become "the people of God, who once were not his [sic] people"(1 Peter 2:10). As such, Christians are perfectly free and yet perfectly

servants to all. Baptism has been well named the sacrament of equality.[9]

If the Church really believes that baptism is God's claiming of each person and is an instrument of equality, then the Church must carefully review its active role in the silencing and estrangement of gay/lesbian Christians and their families and friends. Beyond silence and estrangement, the community of faith also needs to acknowledge its role in the promotion of hatred and division. Remembering the nature of baptism also empowers gay/lesbian Christians because they are reminded that God has acted and claimed them as children of God. Our congregations cannot act as gatekeepers because we are already a part of the Church and the remnant of the faithful. Baptism reframes the dilemma for the church: The questions can no longer be about homosexuality but about the church's failure to live out the gospel, a gospel in which all persons are fully welcome within the community of faith.

Baptism is the initiating rite of acceptance and new beginnings. It is the mark of our equality and the loss of labels and fears. According to Laurence Hull Stookey, "Through baptism, God reveals to us our identity as redeemed creatures."[10] Baptism is the means of grace, justice, and hope that begins our journey, and it is the start of our following of Jesus Christ as disciples. Unfortunately, the first step of the spiritual journey of gay and lesbian Christians often becomes entangled and distorted by the homophobic sin of the church. Our identity is disclaimed and often soiled, and inevitably, we begin to believe God's grace and God's covenant could never be meant for us. The light of hope dims in our hearts and in our souls.

Holy Communion and Its Importance

Almost every Sunday, many mainline Christians will find themselves at the altar table, sharing as a community in the meal of bread and wine that is commonly called Holy Communion, the Lord's Supper, or the Eucharist (coming from the Greek word "eucharista" which means "giving thanks to God"[11]). They come in hopes of strengthening their ties to one another and to God as a community of faith. And whether they can voice it or not, they are hoping to hear again that God has claimed them as they are, as God did at their baptism. Thanksgiving is offered for the community and for the created self. It is here in the drinking of wine and the eating of bread that the community of faith will pray and offer themselves in thanksgiving, and in turn receive God's grace and hope. It is also here that these people will remember God's saving works—and in fact remember the gift of Jesus the Christ. For the majority of Christians this is the most common form of public worship, as it is repeated, unlike baptism, over and over again.[12] At the rail, tears fall and wounds begin their healing. At this table, one engages in self-reflection and often finds new direction. It is here that the people of God dine together in a great feast of grace and hope. At the table of God, we continue to proclaim our following of a Savior who demands sacrifice and expects equality and justice.

Holy Communion is the communal meal in which the community of faith and love shares in the bread and wine, which serve as active symbols of the body and blood of Christ. These elements are a means of grace in which we recognize that God is with us and that God's love is unconditional and available to all people, regardless of gender, race, creed, marital status, financial portfolio, or sexual orientation. By receiving the bread and the one cup, we envision God's grace, but we also realize that we take the sacrament as one body, a community of equality. No one holds a ticket to the seat closest to God's throne. We all are equal in God's sight. It is in the taking of this bread and wine that we really do celebrate the presence of the saving and liberating Christ in our lives. Often, as I administer the sacrament to hurting people or to those who are gay or lesbian in our church, I feel a real presence of the Christ and the active grace of God. Communion not only concentrates on the present moment but also points to the reign of God in which God's love and justice will be known fully. Communion calls us to be people of the gospel that sets us free from hiding ourselves, our pain, and our needs. It delivers the entire community of faith from a myth of lying and living as incomplete creations of God in order to preserve an institution and human doctrine. The bread and wine liberates the Church from the binding cords of exclusion and bureaucracy to a new and exciting vision of ministry and mission. The body of Christ no longer wastes its energy and gifts in the effort to silence and estrange people, but uses its God-given resources to help all of God's children—including gays and lesbians—realize their fullest potential and calling. As James White reflects, "The Eucharist is one of God's greatest gifts to humanity. It is a gift to be received with awe and wonder."[13]

Memory, too, is integral to the sacrament of Communion. It is here that we really do remember. In fact we actually are asked to "Do this in remembrance of me (Luke 22:19)." The bread and wine remind us of a broken body and shed blood. They actively convey to us again the fact that our God experienced the injustice and hatred of humanity on this earth. To remember in the act of taking bread and wine, body and blood, is to remember that our God knows the suffering and abuse of all God's children, including those who are gay/lesbian. In some ways, the body and blood become symbolic of our own sacrifices offered in the prison cells of the Church.

Do This in Remembrance of Us: The Sacraments As a Means of Justice

As we have seen above, the sacraments of Holy Communion and Baptism powerfully shape the experience of the Christian community. They are significant to the spiritual formation and faith development of every Christian. They are the embodiment of hope, grace, and justice. How, then, can the Church of Jesus Christ continue to ignore gay/lesbian Christians and the alienation and exclusion they have encountered in their Christian lives? The sacraments convey God's justice, and in turn, call us to live as a just and inclusive Church. To exclude or degrade any child of God is to desecrate the sacraments and endorse self-righteous bigotry instead of love and acceptance.

James White defines justice in the context of covenant love as " 'a recognition of the personhood of each [human], a refusal to consider any person as of less human worth than any other, and a refusal to reduce anyone to the status of mere means to the good of all the rest. . . . Justice is the expression of covenant love in situations in which rights are involved and a proper balance must be found between competing claims' . . . Justice is also an expression of love."[14] Justice is evidenced by the act of seeking acceptance, inclusivity, and equality in the whole context of God's love and grace. Unfortunately, the sacraments sometimes have functioned as great instruments for reinforcing relationships that are oppressive and unjust. When the Church forbids people to partake because of their known sexuality or forbids them to express who they really are at the table or at the font, the sacraments are compromised. At the same time, the sacraments can be vital vessels of transformation and liberation based on the equality of the baptism, and the communality of the Eucharist.[15] As James White so eloquently states in regard to the issue of the ordination of women, "Churches that refuse ordination to women, if they are consistent, would also deny them baptism."[16] In the same context, if exclusion of gays and lesbians is so crucial to the church, pastors may need to heavily screen all those people who are waiting for baptism, and infant baptism could never be performed again because "you never know." The Church would need to create interrogation sessions for its laity and clergy as a continual monitoring service. How, then, could the Church ever be a witness to God's grace?

Remembering is a vital part of both sacraments. The very ritual of Baptism demands that we continually remember our baptism and be thankful. The ritual for Holy Communion asks us to eat bread and wine in remembrance of Christ and the sacrifice of his body and blood, and to be thankful, as seen in The Prayer of Great Thanksgiving. As we seek justice in our churches and demand a fully inclusive church for all people, especially gay/lesbian Christians, we must remember the just nature of both sacraments. We must remember that each is God's act, not our own. Yet we are called to seek justice and equality in the midst of the sacraments. We must remember that gay and lesbian people are fully children of God, and are equally and beautifully made in the eyes of God. We must work as a baptized, grace-filled Church to guarantee an end to the homophobic sin that plagues our congregations and slashes the hearts and souls of our gay brothers and lesbian sisters in Christ. Hear the call of gay and lesbian Christians—that in remembering our baptism and in partaking of the bread and wine, we remember God's covenant and promise to love. Baptism and Communion represent God's presence in our lives and God's relationship with us through Christ. That presence and relationship sustains and nurtures gay and lesbian Christians as well as the entire community of faith during our most hurtful and troubling hours.

I remember that I am God's. I know that I have not been abandoned by my Creator. When the bishop says that I am not worthy of ordination, when the church says I do not belong, and when my family says I am a total embarrassment, I can only fall back on the one absolute. I belong to God; God has claimed me and will not let go. I am not alone. And God will see me through this journey even if my bishop, my church, my mother, my father, and everyone else sees fit to leave me alone in the unknown. Remembering that promise is a blessing of life and hope.

When we remember, we can do nothing less than be thankful. In our thanksgiving, we must seek sacramental justice for gay/lesbian people as well as other groups that have been hurt and excluded by the church. The prophetic witness of gay and lesbian Christians serves the church well by reminding us to remember and to offer our gratitude . . . and then to act as children of God.

O blessed body of Christ, do this in remembrance of us, of our suffering and tears, of our bashings and fears, and of our deaths. Do this in remembrance of us, of our gifts and our talents, of our hopes and joys, and of our living in Christ. Remember, please remember, and be thankful.

NANCY

"Let's do the time warp again!" The lyrics to the cult movie "Rocky Horror Picture Show" kept drumming through my head. I squatted on my heals, my back holding up the corridor wall. It was the first day of the Spring, 1992 semester at Solano Community College. I felt awkward, old. Was it "uncool" to be seen poking holes in my campus map to fit it into my binder? I chided myself. "You're thirty-seven years old. You are an intelligent, creative woman taking some courses for your own enlightenment. Who cares what's uncool on college campuses? You walked off the Texas Woman's University campus in Denton sixteen years ago. What's your problem?

I could not quite put my finger on the feeling. It was worse than bittersweet, more like a medicine of horseradish and cough syrup. I retired to the restroom to meditate. There, in the stall, I saw the writing on the wall—or, more precisely, on the napkin disposal. A sister had scrawled two interlocking women's symbols and the words "It's natural." This cry for understanding had evoked a plethora of responses, mostly centered around the impossibility of personal fulfillment without the presence of a penis.

Finally, I recognized what had bothered me in the hallway. My mind time-warped to the spring of 1975, to that other college campus: A naive sophomore lay, fully clothed, in the soft arms of a more naive senior. We were stealing a few forbidden, intimate moments. While we longed to lose ourselves in the other worldliness of new love, a corner of our minds stayed alert to the slightest sounds. The rattle of a key in my dorm room door sent us leaping apart like acrobats. We grabbed notebooks and texts to feign study. My roommate whirled in and out of the room. We exhaled.

Our love longed to be shouted from the university clock tower. I wanted to stroll hand in hand with her along campus paths strewn with

redbud blossoms. Most of all, I wanted to talk about her the way another young woman might tell her friends about her new beau: their
first date, their first kiss, their first. . . .

Sandy and I were both virgins when our friendship blossomed into
love. We had no role models and no experience. Cautiously, tenta-
tively, we used our imaginations and taught each other how to fall in
love. We never had the luxury of dating each other; we were not even
likely candidates for a friendship. One morning as we climbed the hill
from our dorm toward campus, I realized that anyone who knew us
would wonder at us walking up a hill together. Sandy was a member
of the elite Aglaians, a literary social club which was, in fact, literally
social. They majored in partying and minored in campus leadership.
In contrast, having rebelled against Catholicism, I enjoyed a seat on
the Executive Council of the Southern Baptist Student Union. We were
taught to preach the gospel, but never to be "unequally yoked" in
friendship, much less romance, with such heathens as the Aglaians.
But God knows no boundaries. On that welcoming spring morning,
Holier-Than-Thou and Heathen traipsed side by side up the hill.

The day after her graduation, I said good-bye to Sandy. Something
told me I would not see her again for a long time. Our parents found
out about our love—they spat out the word as if it were dung in their
mouths—and threatened to disown us if we ever communicated again.
The heat of that Texas summer could not compare to the emotional
hell that consumed our lives. For twenty years I had been respectful
and compliant. Until Sandy, nothing had been worth fighting for. I became a Jekyll-and-Hyde to my mother and father. They were my symbols for a hostile world, versus me, a lone, trapped animal. When I attacked them, I went for the jugular. I secretly read newspaper accounts
of Sgt. Leonard Matlovich, the decorated, gay military man who was
the first to sue the army for discriminatory dismissal. I drew some comfort in knowing that another lone wolf was fighting back.

My parents also had no role models, no positive resources to guide
them through this desperate time. They cajoled, wept, threatened, and
indulged me in their loving, urgent attempt to save me from myself. I
had failed to read the fine print when they promised to finance my college education: " . . . unless you happen to be Queer." My mom put it
this way, "You might as well get used to slinging hamburgers. No one
will ever hire a faggot for a real job." Deep in the heart of Texas in
1975, her fears for me had one foot in reality. I borrowed $100 from
my parents, landed three part-time jobs, and signed up for a full load
of junior-level classes.

It was one of those starched gingham, Texas October afternoons. A Yankee would think it was still summer time. I cut across the grass toward my dorm, where I retreated after work and classes each day to roll tears into the wounds that would never heal. Suddenly, I realized that whether or not I ever saw Sandy again, I was and always would be a Les-bi-an. I shook my fist at the sky, at the male, power-mongering God of my youth. "How dare you do this to me! All I've ever wanted was to be 'normal.' I've always been different. I'm sick of it."

The traffic and milling students moved as if in slow motion in a silent movie. I heard a voice booming around me and within me. "Who are you to tell me what to make?" A passage from Isaiah flashed into my mind, "Shall the pot tell the potter what fashioneth thou?" A wave of fathomless peace washed over me. A gentle voice in my mind's ear reassured me, "It's going to be more wonderful than you can imagine. Just trust Me."

Meanwhile, Sandy busied herself in a frenzy, avoiding her empty apartment in Houston. Loneliness, depression, and her inability to cook had left her skinny and sallow-eyed. Though she had never been one to pray outside of a church, she surrendered me and our future, together or apart, to God. The days, weeks, and months slowly ticked by. On a January day, eight long months since I had last felt the warmth of her touch, Sandy sat working at her desk at Shell Oil Company. She heard a voice that came from nowhere and from everywhere. It said simply, "You may go back to Nancy now."

On Valentine's Day, 1995, Sandy and I celebrated our twentieth anniversary. We are both part of my extended family of sisters, brother, in-laws, nieces, and nephews. While my parents still wish we were heterosexual, they love us both. Sandy's brother and sister have gradually built relationships with us, thanks to her sister-in-law, who had grown up knowing a gay uncle. Sandy's parents disowned her and changed their locks. Eleven years later, letters were followed by brief, awkward visits. Still, they refused to meet me. Finally, in order that Sandy's entire family might celebrate Christmas, 1993 together, her parents tacitly conceded to dine in my presence. Her father now makes light conversation with me when he calls Sandy. Miracles are sometimes wrestled into existence by dogged determination and an open heart.

We have dedicated our lives to helping others to love themselves as the Potter has fashioned them. Despite moments when the kiln has seemed hotter than we could endure, our life together has, as promised, been more wonderful than we could have imagined.

My mind time-warped back to that awkward first day of the Spring, 1992 semester. A line had formed outside the small restroom stall. I heard the roll and clunk of the paper towel dispenser, and I saw a pair of feet impatiently shifting their owner's weight. Before relinquishing my throne, I whispered a prayer for the woman who had scrawled her epistle on the disposal. I asked that her life may become more wonderful than she can now imagine. Stand proud, sister!

PHILLIP

The word around campus was that one day he might be a possible candidate for the office of college president. It was also said that the week following his election as student body president, the college president, an avowed bigot, went into hiding.

There were a lot of hopes and dreams placed on the shoulders of this soft-spoken young preacher. In fact, the college administration offered him a lucrative graduate school scholarship in exchange for his signing a seven-year contract to return to the campus as Assistant to the Vice President for Campus Affairs. How could he turn down such an opportunity and blessing?

When his college pilgrimage began, all he had hoped to do was get a degree, go to some church, and preach the rest of his life. Now he was faced with all kinds of opportunities to do all kinds of things and meet all kinds of people. It was more than a dream come true. But there was only one problem.

After arriving at graduate school, this "rising star" had to face an issue that he had never really confronted with any depth. He liked men. No, he loved men! And at this West Texas football-crazed college campus there were plenty of them to go around. With this being the case, the young preacher sought therapy.

Luckily enough, one of the professors in the psychology department was an expert in the area of homosexuality studies. He had done his Ph.D. dissertation on this subject. This had to be an act of God, being placed within the listening ear of an expert in the field. After months of weekly meetings—and the beginning of a love relationship with a freshman on campus—things did not seem to be coming to any great resolution in the area of sexuality and sexual identity. All he longed for now was a return to his alma mater to do what he knew God was calling him to do.

One of the things this young man of the cloth prided himself on was his honesty and openness. That is probably one of the reasons why, when he returned to his alma mater for spring break, he chose to disclose his sexual struggles with someone he loved dearly, his future boss. How was he to know that with one simple statement, "I am struggling with homosexuality too," he would be banished from the campus and the church? How could he have known that he would be called "deceitful, dishonest, and untrustworthy"? How could he have known that he would be called on to expose other possible "homos"? He couldn't have known. He didn't know. And so he paid the price for his lack of knowledge in this matter. And what a price he did pay.

Upon returning to graduate school to finish a degree program without any real sense of purpose in doing so, he found himself drinking himself into an alcoholic stupor some nights just to get to sleep. He continued his church activities as best he could. He continued seeing his friend. Because the department chair had befriended him, he was allowed to stay at the school a second year to teach as a graduate assistant. These were some of the darkest and most meaningless days of his entire existence—all because he shared the truth.

A lot has happened since that trying period, but we won't go into that here. We will just say that the ones who turned him away "meant it for evil, but God meant it for good."

It has been about fifteen years since I was ousted from this "Christian college" and the Church of Christ. It has been a journey of pain, bewilderment, and growth. Looking back from where I stand and live today, my ouster was one of those death and resurrection experiences that one has in life. From this tomb of pain and despair, over a period of time, a new creation was resurrected.

Needless to say, for some time following the rejection I experienced, I tried to hold on to the dreams I had of being with a Christian school and being a part of the church. I became aware that the word that I was gay was out around the country. This was made clear when I applied for a position with a Christian high school in Georgia. For several months there was a continual, positive corresponding between me and this institution. Then one day, it just ended! It was not until a year later that I was told by someone who had been called to check out my background that one of my references had informed them about my sexuality. I later confronted him in a roundabout way and he acted as if nothing had happened.

Over a period of time I gave up on working with a school and being in the Church of Christ. That period lasted about four or five years. I moved to Dallas and continued to hold on, not as tightly as before, to the idea that somehow God was going to use me in some capacity at a school and a church. But that was just a pipe dream.

After a failed try to return to the church of my youth, back home in Memphis, I was convinced by a friend to move to Dallas. In a matter of days I moved and began looking for employment. After a month of scouring the city, I was hired by Southwestern Bell Telephone Company. This began a new phase of life for me: coming out.

While at Bell Telephone I became acquainted with a number of lesbian and gay employees. Naturally I struck up friendships with most of them. It was during this time that I also met a woman to whom, after four years of dating, I would become engaged. It was definitely a time of ambivalence and searching.

In my third year with Bell it became clear to me that I did not want to wake up one day thirty years down the road and ask myself, "Why the hell have you done this with your life?" With that realization I began to explore my options for returning to my first desire, to be in ministry. Following a year of internal dialogue and discussing the possibilities of seminary with a couple of college friends who were seminarians, I offered my resignation. Looking back, this was one of those giant steps of faith for me—one that I have not to this day regretted.

Another step—maybe more of a leap—of faith I experienced in this time was my engagement to a woman, and the subsequent breaking off of this engagement.

Four years of being honest about my sexuality, and the acting out of my sexual desires, had not deterred this most amazing woman from her vision of being my bride. With her persistence and my need to put on a more secure mask for the church to accept me, I succumbed to the idea of marriage. It was not until after we had reserved the chapel at seminary and ordered her wedding dress that I began to question what we were about to do with, and to, our lives.

In the last months of our time together we moved in with each other. With cohabitation many things surfaced, one of which was my inability to be faithful to this woman. With repeated confessions of unfaithfulness and repeated forgiveness on her part, I decided that we really needed to revisit this idea of being wedded. After months of dialoguing and arguing she agreed to seek premarital counseling with me.

It must have been an act of God that the counselor we were referred to was a white female who was a member and officer in the Church of Christ in DeSoto, Texas! This was a miracle. I will never forget Maggie Shepherd.

Following about a month of lifting up and dealing with all sorts of peripheral issues, one evening I came to the point of why we were seeing her. "Maggie, I'm gay and that's what this is all about!" With these words our therapy took a completely different turn. The three or four sessions that followed were difficult, but productive. Then one evening we walked in and Maggie said, "I suggest you not get married at this time." These words brought me comfort I had not felt for over a year; the same words cut my fiancee's heart out.

As a part of dealing with her grief, the next morning my fiancee called my mother long distance and told her everything. This was my coming out to mom. My mother insisted that things could change if only I would "fast and pray." I said to her, "If you only knew how much I fasted and prayed for this to change when I was in high school you wouldn't even fix your mouth to say those words!" With this we began our long journey of reconciliation, intimacy, and grace.

Today I continue that journey with everyone who I am blessed to touch and who touch me. We, God and I, have come a long way since that day I was rejected at my alma mater. It is an understatement to say that "I stand amazed in the presence of Jesus the Nazarene" when I look back over where God has brought me from. What is so special about where I live today is that with each passing day, my wondering how he could love me diminishes and I find myself just basking in the wonder of his love.

The days of fragmentation and alienation are becoming few and far between. It has been so difficult and painful to try and pull all of the pieces together, especially since so many people I have cared about have told me some of those pieces don't belong. Someone said being black wasn't good enough; another said being gay wasn't right; someone else said you don't cut it in this way or that. I am very certain that if I had returned to my alma mater I would be lost today! I would be a fragmented shell of a human being. Thank God for closing a door and opening up a universe!

At one time, I seemed to aimlessly wander in a search of a place to minister. I now understand that that aimless wandering was leading me to a place I could not have even imagined being in. In recent years and days I have had the privilege of walking with some of the most amazing people on earth: the oppressed of the oppressed, persons living with HIV/AIDS. Some of these fellow pilgrims have allowed me into the sacred places and moments of their lives, and I have been blessed beyond measure. Through these experiences I have come to see more clearly what Paul meant when he said, "Death where is your sting, grave where is your victory?" These little giants have shown me how to live in the midst of suffering and death. They have shown me how to hope when all seems hopeless. This is a gift I could not have asked for, a gift that only unbounded love could supply.

Today I claim and cherish all the paths I have traversed on my journey of being. The paths strewn with the dead leaves of fallen friends and loved ones, those in which the storms of life buffeted me, the paths that seemed dark and ominous and those that offered a mixture of sun and shade . . . all of these have brought me to this glorious moment in my life. All of them have led me to me, and I praise God for me!

5 ◆ And Be Thankful

Do not let the foreigner joined to the LORD say,
    "The LORD will surely separate me from his people";
and do not let the eunuch say,
    "I am just a dry tree."
For thus says the LORD:
To the eunuchs who keep my sabbaths,
    who choose the things that please me
    and hold fast my covenant,
I will give, in my house and within my walls,
    a monument and a name
    better than sons and daughters;
I will give them an everlasting name
    that shall not be cut off.

And the foreigners who join themselves to the LORD,
    to minister to him, to love the name of the LORD,
    and to be his servants,
all who keep the sabbath, and do not profane it,
    and hold fast my covenant—
these I will bring to my holy mountain,
    and make them joyful in my house of prayer;
their burnt offerings and their sacrifices
    will be accepted on my altar;
for my house shall be called a house of prayer
    for all peoples.
Thus says the Lord GOD,
    who gathers the outcasts of Israel,
I will gather others to them
    besides those already gathered.

                        (Isa. 56:3–8)[1]

Marjorie Procter-Smith asserts:

> Thus the rite of baptism does not accomplish the equality it
> is witness to, but it is prophetic and empowering. It calls the
> community forward continually in the struggle to realize its
> own baptismal character as a community of equals "in
> Christ."[2]

When I had gone into class one summer day, the sun had been
shining. When I emerged from the basement classroom, I joined my
peers' moaning and groaning at the sight of the downpour outside.
We all knew that summer thunderstorms in this muggy part of Texas
did not easily roll in and out; we were faced with getting drenched
outside or camping out all afternoon in the doorway.

I sized up the situation, decided against trying somehow to shelter myself with books or newspaper, stuffed my shoes into my back-
pack, and walked out to experience the rain. I was soaked to the skin
in seconds; but I felt happy as my feet splashed in the puddles that
were quickly turning into small lakes. I had to smile at the others who
ran passed me trying unsuccessfully to stay dry. By the time I
reached my car and dry shelter, half a college campus away, I felt ex-
hilarated, alive, my senses renewed. I stopped to ponder the deeper
lesson that I often tried to squeeze out of any experience in those
days. It came to me clearly.

We face many storms in life. We stand in the doorway, smelling
the rain yet grimacing at the interruption of our best laid plans. We
look, and we choose. We can avoid the storm. We can try to protect
ourselves from the experience. Or, we can walk right into the torrent
knowing that there we will experience life, both pain and joy, and
there we will find ourselves again. Our senses will be sharpened. Our
eyes will be opened in new ways, and maybe—just maybe—joy and
thankfulness will well up in us to overflowing. Maybe—just maybe—
we will reexperience "God with us," and we will reconnect with those
around us. Maybe—just maybe—we will remember our trust in God
and what it means to walk by faith together through the storm.

Gay and lesbian Christians, we can walk through the storm.
Though the walk may be long and rocky, and our burdens heavy, we
can walk together. We can be a sign to a Church that has forgotten
what it means to trust, what it means to love, and what it means to
do justice.

Pastor, you may think that the storm of homophobia brewing out
there in your congregation may be too threatening to enter. You hear

the thunder and you see the lightning, but can you stand in the doorway and watch the opportunity to walk with the liberating Christ pass you by? Yes, your walk will not be easy or your burden light, but you are not alone. Come out into the rain; remember your trust in God; remember Christ's embodied stand for justice.

Church member, have you been silent about your loved one who has been turned away, rejected, despised in the name of Christ? Forget your umbrella, it won't do you any good in this storm, but come on out where you can see the rainbow in the distance. The winds are blowing, the hail is beating, and it is a long way to the car, but can you do any less and continue to go to the House of Unconditional Love? Tell the stories, cast out the shame, love God's children, and seek justice.

We hear God's word.

> He has told you, O mortal, what is good;
>   and what does the LORD require of you
> but to *do justice,* and to *love kindness,*
>   and to *walk humbly with your God?*
> (Mic. 6:8)

We have come through the waters of baptism. Our ancestors in the faith came through a parted sea. Can we not walk into the storm and believe that we too will be delivered? We have a responsibility as Christians, dripping wet with the waters of baptism. We are called to seek justice. We are called to live out the baptismal vision.

Make no mistake: Fighting homophobia and heterosexism will not be easy. These forces have kept gays and lesbians silent for hundreds of years. They have fueled innumerous hate-filled sermons and caused beatings, rapes, and murders. People have lost child custody rulings, gainful employment, fair housing rights, as well as the basic civil rights of life, liberty, and the pursuit of happiness.

For non-gay pastors who fight for justice, careers in the church have been halted or derailed. Congregations have been divided. Funding has been jeopardized.

We stand in the doorway and not even the fresh scent of rain could lure us out into the violent storm. But the promise of the new creation can.

> Thus says the LORD,
>   who makes a way in the sea,
>   a path in the mighty waters,

who brings out chariot and horse,
   army and warrior;
they lie down, they cannot rise,
   they are extinguished,
     quenched like a wick:
Do not remember the former things,
   or consider the things of old.
I am about to do a new thing;
   now it springs forth, do you not perceive it?
I will make a way in the wilderness
   and rivers in the desert.
The wild animals will honor me,
   the jackals and the ostriches;
for I give water in the wilderness,
   rivers in the desert,
to give drink to my chosen people,
   the people whom I formed for myself
so that they might declare my praise.
                            (Isa. 43:16–21)

We can choose to stay inside, out of the rain, in the shelter of our homophobic and heterosexist sanctuaries, but soon those sanctuaries turn into closets of dry, parching death. New life cannot pry open its doors. We miss the storm, but we also miss the journey of faith. Our words lose their meaning; our worship becomes deceitful.

We can choose the storm. We can join hands and walk directly into the headwind. We must walk with wisdom, discernment, courage, passion, and purpose. We must trust God. And we must not stop until all are safely on the other side. Along the way, we will come alive again, laughter will find us, and we will be thankful. Let us remember our baptism and be thankful.

Let us consider the possibilities of a church that faces its investment in heterosexism and homophobia by dismantling the barriers to sexuality, relationships, and trust—a church that risks to create a safe place where all Christians can be truth-tellers, to open all the closet doors and do some spring cleaning. This church will create an open community so that the dysfunctional search for intimacy will no longer be encouraged by the church's complicit silence; it will be a place where all can grow in self-discovery with the support of a community that calls each to self-love rather than self-destruction. This church will build on the cornerstone of the liberating Christ, nurturing mutuality, trust, empowerment, community, and embodied faith. Remembering the baptismal call for equality, let us focus on ways the Church can work toward justice for gays and lesbians, growing together in faithfulness and kindness and humbly opening up to the spirit of thankfulness.

Do Justice

◆ *Challenge Those Who Sow Hatred*

Often mainline churches are not intentional proclaimers of hatred for gays/lesbians. Many pastors and church members fall prey to plain old denial, thinking that homosexuality is just an issue that the media has cooked up or that politically correct proponents want to force upon them. While mainline churches may feel that they sit in the middle, if not to the side, of the debate, there is a cacophony of voices sounding out a distorted witness to the Christian faith. Gays/Lesbians live with a bombardment of hatred fed through media outlets and church pulpits, but what we hear from God when we really listen is very different, for God speaks love, peace, and grace. Let us imagine God's response to the Sowers of Hatred, then wonder what God speaks to gays/lesbians. The following is one lesbian woman's reflection.

An excerpt from a Divine love letter (or, An answer to prayer)

To the Sowers of Hatred:
I speak to you as I spoke quietly to the Prodigal Son's Brother.
Do you resent that I love gays and lesbians as I love you? Do you resent that I do not find gays/lesbians guilty of the sin of which you accuse them? Do you resent that I anger over hatred and prejudice and exclusion? Have you kept my lesbian/gay children from coming to me by your own hatred and fears; do you still demand to be in control?

Do not I now offer you an opportunity to do justice, love kindness, and walk humbly with me?

Will you see it, will you see an opportunity to grow in the faith? Will you grasp this spiritual test, this test of humility, this test of seeing others with my eyes rather than with your own cultural stereotypes? Will you see the gay/lesbian creation that I have given to further show the vastness of the world's design?

Will you refuse your brother and sister because you have been taught that to hate is better than to love? What are you afraid of, being left out yourself, not being good enough? No, by my grace you know that you are valued . . . but you would deny that grace to those who are different from you on just that basis . . . *difference* . . . you take my Word (as you call it) and pound my children into the ground . . . their days are spent in silent revolution or screaming protest or painful perishing while you sit in the wealth of your righteousness playing judge and king and lawmaker and law keeper . . . how dare you!

Hear my thunder:
do justice
love kindness
walk humbly.

Let my people go! Let them run free to rejoice in my creation. Let them be free to fulfill their destiny. Let them be free to teach you, to help you understand the pain and death that you have caused so many. . . .

But you sit idly.

You sit to protest that what you think that I tell you is wrong.

Have you sat in silence? Have you sat in silence waiting to know your destruction, praying to be changed, fearful to utter a word of your innermost stirrings? Have you sat in sheer terror over your self-identity? Have you struggled to change? Have you sought with every breath to deny yourself, only to find out that was not what I required at all, no, not at all? No, the author of Love does not call for self-destruction.

Again have you sat in silence as my gay/lesbian children have?

To Gays/Lesbians:
Waiting for me to speak of death, they heard instead, "Walk, you are not dead, you are alive and I rejoice in your loving, I have given you your loving.

I am grieved that so many of my children hate you, promise me that you will try and teach them, promise me that you won't give up on them as they have on you.

It won't be easy. I know too well their weakness, to tear down the weak to build up their sanctuary . . . if you cannot love them, please be kind, teach them with the kindness that their fear and hatred has driven from their lives . . . teach them that their hairdos and appointment books and Bible clubs are clanging cymbals to my ears, their clanging cymbals are so loud.

I know your pain, I know your protest, I have set you a course that is steep and rocky but you are not alone, seek community, walk together, make a strong chain of many links, tend to it daily, meld it with love and justice and kindness and humility. . . .

In all you do, seek wisdom, seek her power, seek her guidance, know her healing breath, feel her loving dance, touch her fierce fire, gather her unblinking courage, and fight. You fight not only for yourself but for all of life.

Smile, laugh, cry, look, listen, know my presence, count on my comfort, don't give up, for I am with you.

And I am with them, with all of you, and you are all precious though the evil of alienation and estrangement shrouds the core of possibility, the spark of a healthy body. Do justice, love kindness, walk humbly."[3]

In Tyler, Texas, January 8, 1994, we joined hands in silence, remembering Nicolas Ray West, his life and his death. Most of us were strangers to him in life, but sisters and brothers as we knew him in death. Nicolas was brutally murdered for being gay. His torturers, filled with the hate and poison of bigotry and their own estrangement, shot him more times than could be counted by the coroner.[4] In the chill of early January, we gathered where he had been abducted only a few weeks before in this strangely lush, green park to remember the ungodliness of the crime and to shout, "No more death." The cry of the crowd did not raise Nicolas from the dead. It did not guarantee the end to hate crimes. But it did signal the depth of our anguish, the tragedy of this needless and heinous crime.

Only three days later, back in the routine of my office work, a scared friend called to see if I knew anything about an urgent meeting of a particular committee on ordained ministry with which her partner would be interviewing in one week. The topic of this hasty yet important meeting was to be that of defining "self-avowed practicing homosexual." Their urgency was due to the upcoming interviews.

Picture twenty or so self-avowed practicing heterosexual pastors sitting down to define "self-avowed practicing homosexual."[5] Imagine the tension in the room as they discussed interview strategies that would catch the Queers but not open the board to a lawsuit. Feel the sense of loss of those who were outvoted, those who spoke against pressing candidates about their sexual orientation. There were those in the room who recognized the fear, ignorance, and bigotry underlying the group's proceedings, but there were more who did not.

I cry with despair that there are even more people who do not go a step further and see the connection between the church's oppressive acts and the brutal slayings of gays/lesbians. By their works the Church signals that gays/lesbians are less than children of God, are not due even common respect, nor are they worthy of basic civil rights. Why would murderers in East Texas ever question that a gay man should be exterminated? Not when the majority of mainline churches remain silent, or worse, closeted in their own meetings of deceit.

Is the church ready to take responsibility for its complicity in the death of Nicolas Ray West? If mainline churches continue to dilly-dally through their sexuality studies and remain silent about gay/lesbian discrimination while the increasingly loud voice of "Hatred Sowers" promote death for homosexuals, the mainline church has given its stamp of approval. While mainline churches wait around deciding whether or not gays/lesbians are worthy of acceptance based on the church's ruling on the cause of homosexuality or its scriptural standing, homophobic violence is going unexamined and untreated.

The church must take a stand against "Sowers of Hatred." As the rally participants, one thousand in number, gay and non-gay, bowed their heads in prayer, the two or three counter-demonstrators chanted their slogans of the evils of homosexuality, seeming not to stop and seek God over the loss of this young man. Was there a collective public cry of outrage from mainline churches in the area? They were not visible at the rally. To be sure, individual pastors and members may have remembered Nicolas in their prayers, crying silently to God of the injustice, but where was the baptismal call of social justice being answered publicly and as a collective faith community? Was the church standing in the doorway hoping the storm would pass over?

◆ Where Do We Begin?

Not everyone can protest openly at a rally. Some cannot because they do not keep abreast about what is happening in the area in which they live. Others, especially but not exclusively gays/lesbians, do not because of the fear of job loss or the threat of violence. Others may not have made up their own minds about the gay/lesbian "lifestyle," or they have not considered the implications of such a death: that hate can murder and it does not go away unchallenged. Perhaps they just did not know what to do. The Church can be a part of teaching people how to *do justice*.

Recently, I received a flyer from P-FLAG (Parents and Friends of Lesbians and Gays) that lists "ten simple things you can do to make a difference."[6] You or I may not be able to do all of them yet, but we can pick at least one that we *can* do, and start there.

1. Become a member of P-FLAG (or any support group) and join with thousands of people from all walks of life, working to end discrimination against gays and lesbians.
2. Teach your children that being gay or lesbian is simply another means of expressing love.
3. If one of your family is gay or lesbian, be sure to let them know you love them just the way they are.
4. Don't tell anti-gay jokes. You just perpetuate the stereotypes about gays and lesbians.
5. Read our P-FLAG literature and find out more about what it is really like to be a lesbian or gay in our society.
6. Be open with others about having lesbian or gay friends or family. Secrecy breeds shame.
7. If you overhear someone making an anti-gay comment, let them know you don't agree or approve.
8. Write congress to protest any anti-gay legislation as you become aware of it.
9. Encourage open and honest discussion of gay and lesbian issues in your home, workplace, and church.
10. Stand with those who believe that discrimination against anyone is a crime against humanity—take a stand with P-FLAG.

For beginners, the more one does to become familiar with the vast experience of gays/lesbians through participating in our culture—by reading our newspapers and other literature, attending our parades and celebrations, eating out in our restaurants, and listening to our joy and pain, with humility and compassion—the more one can become comfortable and thus open to the many ways to seek justice. However, if our paths do not cross or no relationships are attempted, the fight for justice is impeded. We begin by seeing each other as children of God, remembering our baptism of radical equality, and stepping out into the first drops of rain.

◆ Dismantling Barriers

We have already examined the mainline church's investment in heterosexism by examining the barriers to relationships, sexuality, and trust. Homophobia was also named as a power that deters justice. The church can confront heterosexism and homophobia and must do so in order to fight the social estrangement of gays/lesbians.

The church can work to let go of gender roles that enslave women and men, gay and non-gay. There is no God-sanctioned way to be woman or man, but there is an imperative for the baptized. We have a responsibility to teach equality, "no longer slave or free . . . no longer male and female. . . ."[7] The church must confront its own heterosexism and thus its sexism and open up to the new creation before them. Rejoice in the presence of Queer children and adults that God has created out of great joy; in the same joy God has created non-gays. There is no compulsory heterosexuality in God's eyes. There is a vast, wonderful, diverse creation. As the psalmist writes,

> O LORD, how manifold are your works!
>   In wisdom you have made them all;
>   the earth is full of your creatures.
> Yonder is the sea, great and wide,
>   creeping things innumerable are there,
>   living things both small and great.
> There go the ships,
>   and Leviathan that you formed to sport in it.
>   (Ps. 104: 24–26)[8]

We too can delight in God's wild and free creation.

Husbands and wives, do not be enslaved by roles that a sexist culture may try to force on you. Seek God, let your true gifts and desires arise, be who God has created you to be, seek not to judge by a standard role but by the standard of love, enjoy learning to relate rather than learning to act out a script. Let the liberating Christ set you free.

Clearly, the Church *must* take a lasting stand in opposition to violence against women. Homophobia and heterosexism clearly play into hate crimes against women as women are controlled by threats of violence, lesbian-baiting, and church-approved gender roles. As the Church courageously faces its complicit silence in gay/lesbian opression, it must also take a deliberate stand on radical gender equality.

Finally, the Church can work to embrace sexuality as one of God's loving gifts. Sexuality and spirituality need not be in conflict. We can learn what it means to come back into our bodies and find spirituality rather than deny our flesh in order to be spiritual. When we can accept sexuality in general as a good and joyous gift, we will not be hampered as we seek to cast out the fear of diverse sexual orientations. When we can embody our faith, we come closer to the lived life of God incarnate in Jesus Christ.

To seek embodied faith is to embrace the erotic. Irene Monroe, a Ph.D. student in Religion, Gender, and Culture at Harvard Divinity School, in an essay entitled "The Aché Sisters: Discovering the Power of the Erotic in Ritual," writes of the erotic as divine power. She speaks of how the Aché Sisters seek to heal the traditional schisms: male/female, spirit/flesh, heterosexual/homosexual. The Aché Sisters refer to themselves as Zamis, which is an Afrocentric term identifying "one of the most marginalized and oftentimes invisible groups within the African-American church community: the homospiritual lesbians."[9]

> As Zamis we claim that the freedom to explore the power of the erotic allows us to tap into our own personal divine powers; to appreciate all bodies, male and female, as temples of God, and as vessels to do good works; to accept sex as a divine power for responsible co-procreation and co-creation by choice. We accept all sexual orientations as part of the human continuum, seeing such as the varied images of God living co-creatively in the world . . . We believe that in order for the male/female, heterosexual/homosexual, soul/body splits to cease to exist in our worship, we must begin, as frightening as it seems, to look at those ways in which black church worship is presently neither a safe, sacred, nor liberating expression of the divine, but is a ritual expression of the larger society's racism, sexism, classism, and homophobia.[10]

Mainline churches can heal the splits. Churches can also cast out fear by rejecting the idea that we must have something or someone to fear in order to maintain our identity and feel secure. If we split off good and bad, seeing ourselves as good and normal, making "the other" to be bad and strange, then we lose the reality of the mixture of good/bad, health/disease, in us all; we miss the opportunity to recognize our own areas in need of healing and "the other's" incredible gifts for our lives. Mainline churches have been quick to study the perceived "ills" of homosexuality but slow to study their own disease of homophobia and heterosexism. This pattern can change and will do so when churches begin to heal the splits, cast out the fear, and begin the process of re-membering gay/lesbian sisters and brothers.

◆ Act Up: Inside and Out

Goss writes of another way to do justice. Base communities of resistance[11] can be formed separately from mainline churches. He distinguishes between two gay/lesbian political discourses: reformists who try to reform the church by working from within, and transgressives who "act-up"[12] as an external, active form of social protest against the church's gay/lesbian oppression. Reformist strategies try to "transform existing cultural and political institutions,"[13] transgressive discourse creates a "new language around which to construct gay/lesbian lives, to articulate their identities, to express their freedom, and to resist oppression."[14]

Forming base communities of resistance then becomes a transgressive way of moving to the margins, to exile, in order to reclaim just theology, liturgy, and biblical hermeneutics for gays/lesbians. Goss sees Jesus as an example of one who moved to the liminal spaces in order to critique the religious community and act up for the sake of justice.

> He (Jesus) lived in liminal spaces, those in-between boundaries and categories of first-century Jewish Palestine. Jesus invited the outcasts, the undesirables, and the nobodies of his society to share his vision quest for God's reign. He was a boundary breaker, threatening the social boundaries constructed to privilege some and exclude others. He understood that God's reign could only be perceived from the margins of his society and that it would be created from the liminal spaces.[15]

Like Goss, many gays/lesbians see moving out of their lifelong denominations as their only choice in order to be able to remember their baptism, re-experience God's grace and unconditional love, and have the equal standing called for in their baptism. To stay silently in a local church that does not actively challenge its general denomination's oppression of gays/lesbians is to die a silent death and contribute to the lies. To leave takes commitment to a faith in things that are not seen. To leave with confidence is to recognize the power of Jesus' occupation of liminal spaces and choose the growing pains of the new creation. As one lesbian writes:

> Born to be Queer in a world with a straight order, color-inside-the-lines mentality. To be oneself Queer is to deny the "sacredness" of heterosexuality, it is to color outside the lines, but it is also to feel a bit crazy, a bit wrong or off, all of one's life until a point of world-be-dammed, I'm-not-wrong, I'm-not-off attitude can be grown and owned. The prices one pays for that are lost friendships, jobs, and families just in order to survive—we shake hands with grief each and everyday along the path of resistance until we come to full embrace and self-acceptance.[16]

Groups within mainline churches can draw on the best of reformist and transgressive political strategies. These groups can take time to step into the liminal spaces to examine and confess their own complicity in gay/lesbian oppression, work to transform their own practices, and return with political strategies to push for the radical equality to which baptism has called us. We are not called to be acceptable to the mainstream, we are called to exemplify the radical love and acceptance of the liberating Christ. God's call for equality and inclusion does not stop with those who pass as heterosexuals but for those who are on the so-called fringes.

For example, the "welcoming movements"—such as More Light, Reconciling Congregation Program, and Open and Affirming—draw people out to the margins to see their part in gay/lesbian oppression, strategize for change, and move back into the Church with greater awareness, strength, and purpose. The stepping out enables people to go back prepared to be effective agents of change. These movements are like an oasis in the desert of oppressive denominational structures. They are filled with people who have not given up on the Church but know that churches have given up on the radical equality exemplified in baptism. They affirm that church structures will not change until individuals and local churches change.[17]

Pastors, educate yourselves, experience the gay/lesbian culture, enjoy mutual gay/lesbian friendships, incorporate your shared struggles for gay/lesbian justice into your sermons, Bible studies, and committee meetings. Find parents and friends of gays/lesbians and have an honest dialogue about the Church's complicit silence. Humbly ask for suggestions and volunteers. See yourself as a facilitator, not a director of change.

Church members, don't wait on your pastor. Ask questions, immerse yourself in the cares and concerns of the gay/lesbian community, and find ways to volunteer your time to actively work for change.

Gays and non-gays, build bridges of experience together, strategize on political methods of reclaiming God's baptismal vision. Weep, confess, resist, and proclaim together. Join hands and feel the exhilaration of a journey for justice. Go beyond acceptance to radical equality.

Love Kindness

Carter Heyward asserts:

> As a profoundly relational movement, the coming-out process among gay men and lesbians can be paradigmatic for all efforts toward right and honest relationships . . . it is also about making mutually empowering connections between and among us all, whoever we are. Coming out, we well may be drawn into our power in right relation.[18]

The church can show kindness by co-creating safe places for gay/lesbian Christians to share the gift of coming out of the closet with their church families. This is not a patronizing kindness but a gesture based on mutuality and equality—a relationship built on humility, respect, and the desire for truth-telling and justice-seeking. Co-creating places to come out, gays and non-gays together can begin to realize the baptismal vision of radical equality. Allowing the silence to be broken allows for truth to be spoken. The truth-telling of gays/lesbians can become a catalyst for closet-cleaning for the entire church family. Truth-telling helps us to clear out the relational cobwebs and shed new light on the community's life together.

The personal process of coming out for a lesbian woman or gay man offers insight into the process by which we can all become connected to God's unbounded grace. Gays/Lesbians have apparent obstacles of hatred, rejection, and alienation to overcome, but all people have burdens that keep them from being joyous, happy, and free. We can all learn from the painful yet life-giving process of coming out.

The most powerful step in this process is the self-affirming step toward self-acceptance, what I call *coming inside out.* It is coming face to face with shame, fear, rejection, and self-hatred, as well as the loss of being a valued member of society and even the church. Facing this loss allows one to grieve the passing of a tightly held self-image that was once reflected back by society, and it allows one to count the cost of holding on to the old image: constant pain, anger, and distrust. Facing the demons allows us to move forward to new strength and freedom based not on external sources but from an internal well-spring. It is a Good Friday of the soul, when one feels utter loss and meaninglessness, total isolation and abandonment, but it is the only road to Easter. We experience the resurrection of faith, meaning, goodness, and love as we move through our despair to the other side.

Coming inside out is aided by revealing our sexual orientation to others, but it is primarily a journey of the soul that involves various spiritual and emotional support systems. Writing in a journal, having a group that is committed to hearing your pain, working with a therapist or spiritual director—are all a part of the inner process. The courage to face one's inner turmoil may replace the outward fight for justice for a time, but it is nonetheless significant. In fact, it is essential to long-standing health and wholeness. When we are finally able to stand strong and unafraid of ourselves, we are free to go about doing justice and furthering God's reign.

Truth-telling may bring unwanted exposure to well-guarded and long-kept secrets of a faith community. When women, and sometimes men, bring their stories of abuse to the attention of the community, many times the truth-tellers rather than the perpetrators are perceived to be the problem. Moreover, out gay/lesbian Christians, that is, those who are willing to tell the truth about themselves, challenge the dominant culture's heterosexist ideals. This challenge is not without its pain. The Church must be prepared to stand together with all its members, seeking not the status quo but the status of baptism. Truth-telling does not always lead us down the sunny path; instead, it may lead us into thunderstorms, from which we can learn and find new life. Virginia Ramey Mollenkott writes, "A tremendous outpouring of grace will reward the awareness that overcoming heterosexism (and all the other "isms") is to the immeasurable benefit of us all. Only in this way can we participate in the completion of the body of Christ."[19]

In chapter 2, the manifestations of silencing were presented. One of the greatest costs to a gay/lesbian individual who is deep in the closet is terrible isolation, the sense of utter aloneness that can lead to self-destructive behavior unto death—be it physical, emotional, or spiritual death. It is essential that churches offer a safe place where gays/lesbians can gain a sense of community whether the words, "I am gay (lesbian)" ever exit their mouths or not. At minimum, the Church can move beyond enforcing silence and estrangement and move towards a community of love and acceptance. To love kindness means to be a friend as Jesus was a friend (. . . I have called you friends. . . .[20]) It means to listen with compassion, hear without judgment, and together find ways to mutually and equally work for change. The Church offers empowerment and connection against the psychological trauma of isolation.[21]

The Church is often delayed by the nature versus nurture (by birth or choice) debate, and loses opportunities to walk through the storm with the liberating Christ. Many gay/lesbian Christians are strong enough to move on without the help of the Church, and that is the Church's loss. Listen as one lesbian writes of her journey.

> Nature versus Nurture? How are we nurtured? We're not! We have to seek our own way. We are not delivered. We are in the wilderness, crossing the narrow bridge: coming out to self, coming out to God, coming out to others. . . . Our enemies have not been destroyed, the red sea did not close over their heads. However, we break through oppression to a new sense of faith, self-acceptance, and self-esteem. We emerge as a new creation, fresh from the skirts of God whisking us through what seemed impossible; our faces are bright with the sheen of God's presence, scented by the Spirit's winds of liberation.[22]

The Church too can be filled with new life, energized by a journey of tested faith, but the church must choose to step into the storm, take God's hand in one and our neighbors in the other, and move toward justice for all of God's children. There are many ways to cocreate safe places, but those who hold the power must humbly and genuinely relinquish their privilege of control. A church does not "allow" gays/lesbians into their communion, God has allowed us all into God's presence, and none of *us* are the gatekeepers. As barriers are broken and lines of separation erased, authentic relating can emerge, and healthy ways of sharing power and decision-making may begin to develop. It will not be non-gays allowing gays to come to church, but an awareness of the liberating Christ calling us all to sweet communion, teaching us how to pull together against a heavy yoke, singing songs of faith. A Church of courage can cross barriers of fear to relationships of mutuality, as described by Carter Heyward.

Mutuality involves wrestling more fully to embody friendship. It involves learning to stand and walk together and to
recognize and honor the differences we bring to our common
ground. It requires risking *through* fear, not without it, to be
friends. It means working together on our frustrations, hurt,
anger, confusion, and conflicts. . . . Mutuality is a process of
getting unstuck, of moving through impasses, of coming into
our power together. It is the way of liberation, of calling forth
the best in one another and, in so doing, of empowering one
another to be who we are at our best. . . . Mutuality is the
process by which we create and liberate one another. It is not
only about lesbian or gay relationships . . . it is about heterosexual relating, it is about black-white, Hispanic-Anglo,
and Asian-European relating.[23]

Together gays and non-gays can begin to examine language, liturgy,
social-structures, and church polity to transform the Church's life into
an inclusive community.[24] Gays/Lesbians can share their gifts and
talents; gay and non-gay alike, children and youth will be given
gay/lesbian role models, persons who can show the young that they
are not alone and despised but part of God's family and truly cher-
ished. Together, gays and non-gays can seek ways to explore differences honestly without creating lines of estrangement. Rage can offer insights and slowly be defused, isolation can bring its hard fought
lessons and begin to open to community, and self-destructive behaviors can be reformed into self-affirming actions. Distorted theology
can be brought back into focus, and we can celebrate again God's loving act in Baptism.

Walk Humbly

Janie Spahr recalled:

When I go into these churches that have asked me to come
and talk about gay/lesbian justice, I tell them that as long as
there is unequal power, that there really is no dialogue. As
long as they have power to define who I am, we are not on
equal footing.[25]

I resonate with these words, especially as I listen to members of
committees on ordained ministry trying to rationalize their proceedings that seek to define homosexuality. As long as non-gays have

the power to define who gays/lesbians are from their exclusively heterosexual perspective, the balances are uneven. As long as heterosexuals have the power to vote on how they will define what it means to be gay/lesbian, the faith community of the liberating Christ is not making any progress. Gays/Lesbians are still left out of the loop, without a say about their own realities. These heterosexuals assume a knowledge and a right that is not God-given; their words cannot help but be filled with arrogance as well as ignorance.

As long as church structures only allow for heterosexuals to decide how money will be spent in regard to gay/lesbian justice, the baptismal vision of radical equality is only the dry crust of an unused font. When clergywomen conferences or youth camps refuse to have programming for or by openly gay/lesbian Christians because of fear that denominational money will be withheld, the fight for justice ends before it is clearly finished. The courage to press on has lapsed into complacency and fear. Denial has aided rationalization. When churches decide that they do not want to take a public stand for gays/lesbians because they do not want to become a "gay church," the body of Christ becomes measured by mainstream standards rather than by the waters of baptism. The Spirit is quenched. As Carter Heyward asserts,

> Any unequal power relationship is intrinsically abusive if it does not contain seeds both of transformation into a fully mutual relationship and of mutual openness to equality.[26]

Hear again the third movement of Micah's familiar passage: "what does the LORD require of you . . . to *walk humbly with your god.*" Out of humility, a heterosexist and homophobic church can confess its oppression, acknowledge its arrogance, and start on the road toward recovering its baptismal call. In humility, a church can stop its voting and defining and start to listen and learn—not waiting impatiently to interject and offer easy solutions or self-centered comparisons—but to truly listen.

If I were to develop a continuum depicting stages of acceptance by which one can evaluate one's own progress on being a recovering heterosexist, it would look something like the list below. As you read through the continuum, be aware of the progression from "you" to "I" statements and from the term "homosexual" to "gay/lesbian."

1. Awareness that "those homosexuals" or "you people" exist. Fear homosexuals because they are different.

2. Accept homosexuals because they are the stranger, the outcast, or the "other."
3. See some similarities, but mostly see homosexuals as unduly and overly angry, militant, and sensitive. Impatient with their feelings.
4. Assume that you understand the gay experience, know what homosexuals are feeling.
5. Realize that you have silent, unexamined assumptions about gays/lesbians.
6. I've not thought about that before. I don't know everything. I can ask questions.
7. I make mistakes. I cause pain by ignorance. I want to learn, change, and grow. I will need to be corrected.
8. I can learn something new. I am more aware of assumptions that I make. I actively spend time thinking of the different ways of loving in this world.
9. Please tell me when I have hurt you.
10. I need to monitor and correct myself.
11. "I am angry for you" becomes "I am also angry."
12. We can mutually work for justice for all people.

Of course, not everyone goes through each stage. Some people seem to begin at number 4 and over time go back and forth through the other 8, others rarely get past 1, 2 or 3. Few people are fully recovered heterosexists or racists or sexists; we all continue to relearn lessons of appreciation and respect for others. We all have a place to begin, a starting point for truly embracing and valuing diversity, a coming out for our prejudice and oppression.

Coming out is a personal and political act that offers room to live, grow, and express oneself. The Church fears this, though. When we as gays/lesbians grow in self-acceptance and realize what is at stake by staying silent, we have further reason to keep coming out and speaking up. A life-quenching cycle often develops as gays/lesbians come into their personal power; as gays/lesbians come out more and more, they become less and less acceptable in mainline churches. Where a closeted gay/lesbian Christian leader was once welcomed and respected, this leader is no longer welcomed or embraced after moving towards healthy honesty. Once out of the church-imposed closet, they are politely asked not to give of their gifts and talents— often with the empty response, "We're just not ready for you yet. You understand, don't you?"

There is a fear that the everyday oppression that gays/lesbians experience will somehow have to be suffered by "innocent" groups. Gays/Lesbians are asked over and over to understand the slowness of the church and to accept a silent role for the good of the congregation, the kids, the funding, and so on. When we cry out for justice and equality, we are told that we are not being patient. When we speak up for basic civil rights, we are told that we want special privileges. When we seek to be public with our affection, we are told that we are flaunting our sexuality. Of course, we see heterosexuality flaunted everywhere from car ads to toothpaste commercials. Whose problem is this?

> The liberal churches have always displayed some measure of tolerance toward those women and homosexual people whose *public* presence has been strictly in conformity with patriarchal social relations. Passive, self-effacing women, and men and women who have kept their homosexual activities closeted from public knowledge, have been well received, on the whole, throughout christian history. . . . Women and homosexual people pose no practical problem to the church unless we *publicly challenge* the church's sexism and heterosexism.[27]

As Heyward recognizes, there are layers of oppression and hierarchies of power in mainline churches. The reality of limited funds makes many oppressed groups reluctant to take on the fight for a group that is less acceptable. Many women's groups within churches refuse to take on justice issues for lesbians because they would lose their funding. Many pastors in the middle or lower rungs of the church's corporate ladder are also reluctant to risk their relative power on behalf of the powerless. That leaves very few persons to fight safely for justice—persons who have the least amount of risk but have benefited the most from the patriarchal system. However, Pharr points out, "We must keep clearly in mind . . . that privilege earned from oppression is always conditional and is gained at the cost of freedom."[28] Who then is left to fight for justice? Who has the courage to risk loss of privilege?

Pastor Martin Niemoller's familiar meditation may be paraphrased as follows:

> In Germany they first came for the Communists, and I didn't speak up because I wasn't a Communist. Then they came for the Jews, and I didn't speak up because I wasn't a Jew. Then

they came for the trade unionists, and I didn't speak up because I wasn't a trade unionist. Then they came for the Catholics, and I didn't speak up because I was Protestant. Then they came for me—and by that time no one was left to speak up.[29]

Oppressed groups within mainline churches can build coalitions or base communities of resistance to counter heterosexist and homophobic church structures. Base communities can be a place of nurture, strength, and strategy. Coalitions can actively educate themselves and others on the common elements of oppression—the common origin being economic power and control[30]—and work together to dismantle the oppressive barriers. Pharr writes:

> We must find ways to build coalition, to make broad social change for all of us. There are many more people who are considered the Other . . . than those who are defined as the Norm. We must become allies in a movement that works against power and control by the few and for shared power and resources for the many. To do this work, we will have to build a program that provides an analysis of the oppressions, their connections, and together we must seek ways to change those systems that limit our lives.[31]

We hear the ancient call for us to walk humbly with our God as well as to do justice and love kindness. The church cannot continue to avoid getting wet; it is in danger of allowing the waters of baptism to dry in the font and true thankfulness to be a faded memory. The thunder sounds, the lightning cracks, the rains begin to pound; we may all get drenched but we will be alive. Come out into the storm, be immersed again in the waters of baptism, and reclaim your status as a child of God! Remember our baptism and be thankful! Alleluia!

◆ Epilogue

Dear Marilyn,

I cannot believe that we have come to the conclusion of birthing this book, with all of its struggles, difficulties, and joys. I must admit to you that when we first began discussions and later actual writing on this project almost two years ago, I never really believed we would complete—let alone—publish such a project. But I underestimated the power of a friendship that has called me to be honest with myself and my soul, a relationship that kept me from hiding and not believing that I am a child of God. I also minimalized the work of the Spirit in this process, which led me to face my own homophobia and to accept myself and the gift of my sexuality more completely.

I realize, more clearly now than ever, that God has claimed me in baptism, and I am God's child. The Church's efforts to exclude me, my family's hopes that I will change, and the ultimate fear of being out have lost their grip on me. In fact, this book has empowered me to live out God's call with more conviction and integrity than I ever thought possible. I no longer feel great fear or dread about my future or even the future of the Church. I am not naive, for I know the journey will continue to be long and sometimes very difficult. Yet I know that the God who created me as gay is the same God that will guide and protect me as I approach the unknown.

Anger dominated my life in the beginning of this journey. I was so mad at the Church, our society, my family, and even myself that I often found myself emotionally paralyzed as a victim of ecclesiastical hatred, fear, and indifference. In the writing of this book, I found the anger constructively harnessed and rechannelled to an avenue of activism, compassion, and empowerment. The Church can no longer silence or estrange me. Out of my baptism, I can live as an empowered gay Christian. Instead of leaving the mainline church and beginning again, I feel strongly committed to transformation and liberation within my own denomination. No longer am I serving the United Methodist congregation I loved, but I am now in ministry with the Reconciling Congregation Program, a welcoming movement for gay/lesbian persons.

I recall the baptismal water and how it sealed a covenant with God that can never be taken from me, even by a homophobic church. As I remember and am thankful, I now challenge my gay brothers and lesbian sisters to do the same. My hope is that the community of faith will recall the covenant as well. Marilyn, what I am saying is that I now remember my baptism, and I can honestly say I am thankful.

Dear James,

To change or not to change (denominations) was the question that in the beginning focused this book for me. Why, with all the pain, silence, and rejection, did I stay in the United Methodist Church? Why not leave? Why endure silently?

The answer was in my baptism, the sign of God's acceptance, the Church's welcoming party. I stayed because of the many gifts that the Church had given me, including the conviction that we are all children of God. Through the Church, the Spirit had strengthened my resolve to seek justice wherever I saw oppression. I just did not know it would hit home so closely and intensely, that I would be fighting for my own sense of self-worth, my own place in the Church and world.

The journey for me has been in finding my voice. Starting with a halted whisper and moving to the low hum of the computer, I have come inside out of my pain, fear, and estrangement. Sometimes forcing the words out through tears, I have started the cleansing of my soul that had long been thirsty for water. It was hard. It was depressing. It was debilitating.

Somewhere in there though, I turned the corner on my powerlessness. Somehow I made the shift from helplessness to hopefulness. A rush of wind, a breath, formed my first exclamation, "No, you are wrong, I am a child of God. I am loved and I am called to love." Along the way, my mourning did turn to dancing, peace came out of the despair.

Here we are, two years later, preparing to join the chorus of justice seekers. I grab hold of the hands who have gone before us—hands of many colors and stages of life—and hang on tightly, for together our laughter is hardier and our steps not so heavy.

Do justice, love kindness, walk humbly, and always, always make laughter your friend.

◆ Appendix A

Congregational Reaffirmation of the Baptismal Covenant

GATHERING

Brothers and sisters in Christ:
Through the Sacrament of Baptism
    we are initiated into Christ's holy pathway.
We are incorporated into God's mighty acts of salvation
    and given new birth through the water and the Spirit.
All this is God's gift, offered to us without price
    but certainly with great responsibility.

RENEWING OUR UNDERSTANDING OF BAPTISM

On behalf of the whole Body of the Liberating Christ, I ask you:
Do you renounce your participation in the social constructs of
    bigotry, hatred, and marginalization?

I do.

Do you accept the freedom and power God gives you
    to resist evil, injustice, and oppression
    in whatever forms they present themselves?

I do.

Do you proclaim Jesus Christ as your Liberator,
    put your whole trust in his grace,

and promise to work with him in doing justice,
in solidarity with the Body which Christ has offered to all
    people?

I do.

According to the grace given to you,
    will you act as justice-doers and love-makers
    and be the Liberating Christ's disciples in this world?

I will.

THANKSGIVING OVER THE WATER

[*At this time the water may be poured into a large glass bowl in such a way
that those gathered can see and hear the water; and then the following
prayer is offered.*]

The Liberator set you free.

The Freedom of Christ Be Yours Also.

Let us pray:

Eternal Lover,
When nothing existed but chaos,
    you swept across the dark waters and brought forth light.
In the days of Noah
    you saved those on the ark through the water.
After the flood you set in the clouds a rainbow.
When you saw your people as slaves in Egypt,
    you led them to freedom through the sea.
Their children you brought through the Jordan
    to the land that you promised.

[*Sing: "We Shall Overcome"*]*

In the fullness of time you sent Jesus,
    nurtured in the water and the womb.
He was baptized by John and anointed by your Spirit.
He called his disciples
    to share in the baptism of his death and resurrection
    and to proclaim the liberating gospel to all people.

---

*All hymns referred to in this appendix can be found in the *United Methodist Hymnal,* Nashville: The United Methodist Publishing House, 1989.

[*Sing: "We'll Walk Hand in Hand"*]

Pour out your Holy Spirit,
   and by this gift of water call to our remembrance
   the grace and justice declared to us in our baptism.
For you did not silence us or call us stranger
   but led us from our own wilderness times
   into the Promised Lands of self-acceptance and thanksgiving.
You have set us as a rainbow in the sky
   to be a sign of your unending cry for justice and liberation.

Praise to you, loving Spirit, we hear your cry and we respond. We will act-up with marches, singing, and hosannas until your will be done. Amen.

REAFFIRMATION OF FAITH

[*We recommend that those gathered form a circle and the minister/facilitator begin the remembrance by touching the water and making the sign of the cross on the forehead of the person to either the right or left, saying "Remember our baptism and be thankful." That person then takes the water and marks the next person in the circle, repeating the remembrance phrase. After the water has gone around the entire circle and the minister/facilitator has been signed, together the group proclaims:*]

We remember our baptism and we are thankful.
We remember our baptism and we are thankful.
We remember our baptism and we are thankful.

BENEDICTION

Go forth for justice and liberation!

Great Thanksgiving
for National Coming Out Day

The Liberator set you free.

The freedom of Christ be yours also.

Open up your hearts.

We open them up to God.

Let us give thanks to the God who created us.

And the God who nurtured us.

It is right, and a good and joyful thing,
always and everywhere to give thanks to you,
Lover of all people.
Creator of our loving.
Once we were a people living in closeted darkness, fearful of the
truth of our radical loving, ashamed of the image of God that we
embody. Once we waited in the shadows and allowed the church
to silence and estrange us, to tempt us with the fruit of deceit. We
looked on as Queer brothers and sisters were bashed, ostracized,
and murdered for their love-making and justice-doing.

In the presence of our enemies—silence, fear, and violence—you
called us out of our closeted shame and self-pity to be a people of
hope and joy. You transformed the churning waters of oppression, alienation, and isolation into the life-giving waters of our
baptism. Because of your grace and justice, we are no longer a
people of the closet but a people of parades, rainbows, and quilts,
called to lead your church in a march for liberation.

And so, with all your people on earth and all the company of
heaven, we praise your name and join their unending hymn.

**Sacred, wholly liberator, God of our deliverance, blessed is
the one who seeks justice, whose love knows no bounds.**

Loving and holy God, blessed is your child Jesus Christ in whom
your call for grace-giving, love-making, and justice-doing was
embodied.

In his journey to heal wounds of estrangement and silence, to
cast out demons of fear and hatred, Your Spirit anointed him to
act up against all forms of oppression, bigotry, and enslavement.

On the night on which he acted up, he took bread, gave thanks to
you, broke the bread, gave it to his disciples and said, "Take, eat,
this is my body which is given for you. Do this in remembrance
of me and all who act up in my name."

When the supper was over, he took the cup, gave thanks to you,
gave it to his disciples and said, "Drink from this all of you, this is

my blood of the new covenant, poured out for the hope of new life. Do this as often as you drink it in remembrance of me and all who act up in my name."

And so in remembrance of these offerings for justice in Jesus Christ, we offer ourselves as a chosen people to bring the fullness of Your Reign on earth as we proclaim the mystery of faith.

Christ has died. Christ is risen. Christ will come again.

Pour out your liberating Spirit on us gathered here and on these gifts of wheat and vine. Make them be for us nourishment for the way of Christ, so that we may be for the world a beacon to your unconditional love.

Through Christ, with Christ, and in Christ,
in the unity of the Holy Spirit,
all glory is yours, God most holy,
now and forever

Amen.

A Celebration of Coming out

[*This celebration provides the opportunity for a lesbian, gay, bisexual, or transgender church member to ask for and receive support from her or his congregation. This may be done as a part of the Sunday morning worship service or as a special private ceremony.*]

INTRODUCTION

[*A few brief words should be said about the importance and joy of this celebration. The one coming out will stand with the presider next to the baptismal font. The presider will begin as follows:*]

The Liberator set you free.

The Freedom of Christ be yours also.

In keeping with our baptismal covenant to surround this child of God with love, prayer, support, and nurture, will you now stand in solidarity at this crucial step in (her/his) journey?

[The congregation will now stand as they are able, then respond:]

We are with you.

SCRIPTURE OR OTHER SPECIAL READINGS

[Selected readings or scripture passages may be read at this time. Suggested verses: Genesis 1:26–27, Psalm 139:1–16, Isaiah 56:4–5, Matthew 5:13–16, John 16:33, Romans 8:35–39, or Galatians 3:27–28.]

DECLARATION OF COMING OUT

[The one coming out steps forward and declares:]

I praise God for I am fearfully and wonderfully made. Wonderful are the works of God—that I know very well. Therefore, I am proud to say, "I am a *(lesbian/gay/bisexual/transgender)* child of God."

WITNESS

[The congregation is seated. The one coming out may give a brief witness of the faith journey that has brought her/him to this point and/or others may witness to the person's coming out.]

CONGREGATIONAL RESPONSE

[The presider begins:]

(*Name*), we are humbled by your courage, which testifies to your faith in the Liberating Christ.

[The congregation responds:]

(*NAME*), you are wonderfully and fearfully made, and we give thanks to God for your faithful presence in our midst. May we be worthy companions on your journey.

PRAYER WITH LAYING ON OF HANDS

[Friends and loved ones encircle the one coming out and lay hands on the one's head as the presider begins:]

Let us pray for (*name*).

Prayers of the people will be offered.

BLESSING

[*The presider continues:*]

> (*Name*), you are a child of God, a disciple of the Liberating
> Christ. May God bless you as you continue to leave the shadows
> of the closet and walk in the light of truth and freedom. Amen.

HYMN(S) OF CELEBRATION

[*Suggestions: "Child of Blessing, Child of Promise," "I Want to Walk as a
Child of the Light," or "Wash, O God, Our Sons and Daughters"*]

A Ritual of Self-Renewal

[*This ritual is for anyone who seeks to replenish one's spiritual storehouse.
The struggle for Queer justice is an ongoing journey. We recognize that
coming out, acting-up, or facing homophobia (internally or externally) or
any other major milestone along the liberating pathway depletes our spiritual resources. We offer this ritual as a reminder and a means to nurture
and re-energize oneself.*]

PREPARING

> Choose a quiet place that is sacred for you. Bring with you a bowl
> of water, a candle with matches, meditative readings, and your
> journal. You may want to add more elements to your sacred
> space such as music, seashells, photographs, pride symbols or
> religious icons. Arrange your sacred space so that you are
> comfortable and that you are fed by the environment.

> Relax, breathe deeply, and prepare to enter this time of renewal.

NAMING

> Write down those events, persons, or revelations that occupy
> your mind and emotions. This journal entry may be a list, a short

reflection, or a detailed account. Write until you have named all that has exhausted or challenged you.

Out loud, name key names, words, and phrases in an effort to make yourself hear the issues before you. For example, this may be the first time that you admit that you are attracted to persons of the same gender, that you are fearful of gay and lesbian people, or that you are burned out from constantly advocating for gay and lesbian rights.

CLEANSING

Now you are ready to light your candle. As you strike the match and ignite the flame, speak or meditate upon this prayer:

Liberating Spirit, transform the burning rage, the parched loneliness, and the searing pain of my struggle into a purifying flame that brings light, warmth, and wisdom to the shadows of this moment. Create in me a strong spirit.

FILLING

Begin your meditative readings, aware of the nourishment that they offer. Read until your needs are met. Meditating and journal writing may be helpful here.

BLESSING

Place your bowl of water in front of you; feel the sensation of the water as you dip your hands into the bowl and prepare to follow this blessing ritual.

Touch your fingers to your forehead and say:

Bless my thinking with wisdom

Touch your eyes and say:

Bless my seeing with clarity

Touch your ears and say:

Bless my hearing with discernment

Touch your mouth and say:

Bless my speaking with truth

Touch your heart and say:

Bless my loving with honesty

Touch your palms and say:

Bless my caressing with compassion

Touch your center and say:

Bless my being with faithfulness

Touch your legs and say:

Bless my marching with purpose

Touch your feet and say:

Bless my standing with courage

Closing

Extinguish the flame of the candle, and as the smoke rises, lifting your prayers to God, say:

I now go forth in strength and peace. Amen.

◆ Appendix B

Self-Reflection Worksheet

What are you feeling? (Angry, sad, threatened, relieved, sorrowful, enraged, confused, accepted, or _____?)

What triggered these feelings for you?

What new ideas have challenged you?

What old ideas continue to plague you?

What doors has this reading opened up for you?

When you are ready, we hope that you will continue your journey through the book.

◆ Notes

Notes to Introduction

1. Robert Goss, *Jesus Acted Up* (San Francisco: HarperSanFrancisco, 1994), xix.
2. Ibid.
3. *The 1992 United Methodist Book of Discipline* (Nashville: The United Methodist Publishing House, 1992), 76–82.
4. Victor Paul Furnish, "Some Perspectives on the Bible and Homosexuality," in *Christian Argument for Gays and Lesbians in the Military* (Lewiston, N.Y.: Edwin Mellen Press, 1993), 1.
5. Ibid., 3. See also Danna Nolan Fewell and David M. Gunn, *Gender, Power and Promise* (Nashville: Abingdon Press, 1993), 192. Fewell and Gunn state the following: "The category, 'homosexuality,' is generally unknown in the ancient world—probably because it implies a person necessarily having a fixed and exclusive same-sex orientation, something not obvious, it would seem, to many ancients. Furthermore, a strictly essentialist understanding of sexuality is deeply problematic—even though talk of genetic disposition may be helpful in confronting the current bigotry. Sexual orientation might usefully (though not unproblematically) be thought of in terms of a spectrum where no person has necessarily a single fixed place, though genetic determination may constrain that person's range of options."
6. "Their intent was homosexual rape, which (precisely like its heterosexual counterpart) is the dehumanization of one human being by another or, as in this case, others. . . . Nevertheless we must see the sin of Sodom for what it is: it was an attitude of

mind that justified the abuse of one human being by another. It was an attitude that would turn people into objects—things— to be used or abused. This was sinful then and it still is today." Tom Horner, *Jonathan Loved David* (Philadelphia: Westminster Press, 1978), 48, 50. Walter Brueggeman places the sin of Sodom in the turbulence of the narrative. He argues that not only is it a violation of hospitality but the violence of gang rape. He notes that *outcry* in 19:13 argues for an abuse of justice (See Robert Goss, *Jesus Acted Up*, 217).

7. See John Shelby Spong, *Rescuing the Bible from Fundamentalism* (San Francisco: HarperSanFrancisco, 1992), 7. Spong comments further on Genesis 19: "In the Biblical world of male values, the humiliation of a male was best achieved by making the males act like women in the sex act. To act like women, to be the passive participant in coitus, was thought to be insulting to the dignity of the male. This, far more than homosexuality, was the underlying theme of the Sodom story. The hero of this tale was Lot, a citizen of Sodom, who offered the sanctuary of his home to the angelic messengers and who protected them from the sexual abuse of the men of Sodom. Few preachers go on to tell you that Lot protected these messengers by offering to the mob for their sexual sport his two virgin daughters. You may 'do to them as you please'" (Gen. 19:8).

See also Danna Nolan Fewell and David M. Gunn, *Gender, Power and Promise*, 134. Fewell and Gunn add the following words to the discussion of Judges 19: "Finally, an old man, himself a native of Ephraim, takes the tired troop in. While they are relaxing in the old man's house, the men of the city, a worthless lot, surround the house insisting that the Levite be brought out that they might 'know' him. Hardly a welcoming committee, their intent is torture and humiliation, 'sport' at the expense of the Levite. The old man protests, offering him his daughter and the Levite's wife instead. The men, however, are adamant and the Levite, in desperation and no doubt blaming his wife for the situation he is in, seizes her and throws her out to the mob."

8. Lindsey Louise Biddle, "Hospitable Interpretations of Sodom and Gomorrah," in *OPEN HANDS* 9:18–20.

9. Peter J. Gomes, "Homophobic? Re-Read Your Bible," in *New York Times*, August 17, 1992.

10. See Danna Nolan Fewell and David M. Gunn, *Gender, Power and Promise*, 192–93. Fewell and Gunn comment further: "We

seem to be dealing here with the notion of seed as limited resource; there is only so much seed and its owner must not waste
it. Hence Onan in Genesis 38 compounds his crime against his
brother's name and inheritance with deliberate waste. Invol-
untary emissions in the night or during sex with a woman (Lev.
15:16–18) are understandably a different matter and can be
dealt with less drastically."

11. Focusing on the problem of wasting the Israelite seed has become common among scholars (See Norman K. Gottwald, *The
Hebrew Bible* (Philadelphia: Fortress Press, 1985), 477. Gottwald states: "Biblical scholars have been inclined to think that
homosexuality was stigmatized in ancient Israel because of
its practice in Canannite fertility religion; recently, however,
doubts have been raised about whether cult prostitution was
practiced as widely in Israel's environment as once thought.
There is also the real possibility that male homosexuality (les-
bianism is not mentioned in the Hebrew Bible) was abhorred
in ancient Israel because it seemed to involve a prodigal waste
of 'male seed,' which according to ancient misunderstanding
was thought to be limited in quantity or potency. In that event,
to be a homosexual was to be derelict in fathering the large families that were the cultural norm for agricultural Israelites."

See also Jacob Milgrom, "Does the Bible Prohibit Homosexuality," in *Bible Review*, December, 1993, 11. Interestingly
enough, Milgrom suggests adoption as a means for Jewish gay
men to extend their lineage: "To Jewish homosexuals I offer an
unoriginal solution. As compensation for your loss of seed,
adopt children. Although adoption was practiced in the ancient
world (as attested in Babylonian law), there is no biblical pro-
cedure or institution of adoption. As a result the institution is
absent from rabbinic jurisprudence. . . . Thus from the Bible we
can infer the following: Lesbians, presumably half of the
world's homosexual population, are not mentioned. More than
ninety-nine percent of the gays, namely non-Jews are not addressed. This leaves the small number of male Jewish gays subject to this prohibition. If they are biologically or psychologi-
cally incapable of procreation, adoption provides a solution."

See Tom Horner, *Jonathan Loved David*, 85. Horner argues
against the issue being the destruction of the male seed. "If
Tripp and the authorities he cites are correct, then we need not
concern ourselves with the notion that a fear of underpopula-

tion had to do with the Levitical prohibitions of homosexuality. The Levitical writers, of course, did not know what Tripp knows, but they *did know*, far better than we, that married men also engaged in homosexuality and that this had nothing what-soever to do with the number of children that they may or may not have sired. In fact, all men in antiquity knew that. Indeed we are the ones who do not seem to know this about ourselves.

"What we know about these Levitical writers in respect to their aversion to homosexuality is that this aversion was cultic in origin, and that this cultic abhorrence was reinforced by the contemporaneous Persian attitudes, both legal and spiritual."

12. See Victor Paul Furnish, *Moral Teachings of Paul* (Nashville: Abingdon Press, 1985), 71–72. According to Furnish: "We must acknowledge that 'homosexuality' is not the topic in this pas-sage, and that the two words which, taken together, constitute a reference to it, are part of a traditional list of miscellaneous vices commonly attributed by Jews to Gentiles. Paul uses the list as a reminder to his readers that as Christians, they should have put their old ways behind them. There is no indication that he is aware of or has been asked about any particular prob-lem of homosexual practice in Corinth. In fact, the sexual im-morality with which he is specifically concerned in this context is heterosexual in nature (1 Cor. 5:1–5; 6:12–20)."

13. Furnish, *Moral Teachings of Paul*, 68–69. Furnish explains the original text in question: "The two Greek words in question are *malakoi* and *arsenokoitai*. The root meaning of the first term is: 'soft' or 'weak,' and by extension, 'effeminate,' as in some trans-lations of 1 Corinthians 6:9. It is significant that this is the very term the critics of 'call-boys' often use to describe those who of-fered their bodies for pay to older males. That Paul is using it this way here seems likely, because it stands in a list where sev-eral other terms referring to sexual immorality also appear, for example 'fornicators' (RSV renders this term too broadly, as 'the immoral') and 'adulterers.'

"The second disputed term is compounded of the word for 'male' or 'masculine' and a word that refers to 'ones who go to bed.' Its literal meaning, therefore, is something like, 'those who go to bed with males.' Although 1 Corinthians 6:9 is the first documented use of the word, because it is associated here with the term *malakoi* it probably refers to males who engage in sexual activity with other males. Indeed, Robin Scroggs argues plausibly that the word is simply a literal rendering in the Greek or the Hebrew phrase *mishkav zakur,* 'lying with a male,' which was the usual early rabbinic way of referring to male homosexual intercourse. Since *malakoi* would refer to the 'effeminate' or passive partner in such a relationship (thus, 'catamite' in Moffatt's version and the Jerusalem Bible), *arsenokoitai* doubtless refers to the male who assumes the more active role (translated 'sodomite' by Moffatt and the Jerusalem Bible)."

cf. Tom Horner, *Jonathan Loved David,* 100. Horner comments: "Another New Testament reference will confirm the stricture on the *arsenokoitai* or 'pederasts,' of 1 Corinthians 6:9, although this time they are a part of a still longer list and among 'the lawless and obedient' for whom the Jewish law was originally given. . . . (1 Timothy 1:9–10)."

14. See George D. McClain, "What Does the Bible Say about Homosexuality," *Social Questions Bulletin* 83:2–3. See also Victor Paul Furnish in *Homosexuality in the Church,* ed. Jeffrey S. Siker (Louisville, Ky.: Westminster John Knox Press, 1994), 27. Furnish elaborates: "Again, it was presupposed that sexual intercourse requires one partner to be active and the other passive, that nature has assigned these roles to the male and female, respectively, and that homoerotic acts inevitably confuse these roles, thus confounding what is 'natural.' In the case of two males, one was understood to be 'demeaned' by assuming the passive role, thought to be 'naturally' the woman's. In the case of two females, one was understood to be usurping the dominant, active role, thought to be 'naturally' the man's."

15. Robert Goss, *Jesus Acted Up,* 92. See Victor Paul Furnish, *Moral Teachings of Paul,* 78. Furnish writes, "Since Paul offered no direct teaching to his own churches on the subject of homosexual conduct, his letter certainly cannot yield any specific answers to the questions being faced in the modern church."

16. George D. McClain, "What Does the Bible Say about Homosexuality?" See also George R. Edwards, *Gay-Lesbian Liberation* (New York: Pilgrim Press, 1984), 92–93. Edwards elaborates: "To summarize, in the two specific references to same-sex acts in the letters of Paul, they are united with a root cause, idolatry and fornication or adultery. These three components are found in Hellenistic Judaism, especially the Wisdom of Solomon, which is a storehouse of ideas that crop up in Romans 1:18–32 and elsewhere in Romans. The same three ingredients

are also attested in the Deuteronomic history. Paul, therefore, is utilizing a tradition, a tradition especially characterized by Judaism's perspective on gentile depravity. The critical question is, How does Paul regard this threefold tradition? Is it taken up at face value, uncritically, or does Paul use it rhetorically in order to gain the assent of the Jewish boaster whose judgment against the gentiles becomes his own condemnation in Romans 2? In this final section the view is maintained that Romans 1:26–27 stands in a rhetorical context wherein Paul uses a traditional Jewish pattern of ideas directed against gentile depravity in order to turn the accusation against the accuser, just as the prophets turned the ethnocentric accusations against the Canaanites on Israel itself and gave rise thereby to the moral depth of prophetic religion."

17. Victor Paul Furnish, "Some Perspectives on the Bible and Homosexuality," p. 7.
18. Cf. Exodus 16:18–20; Deuteronomy 8; Psalm 82; Proverbs 15:33 and 21:3; Isaiah 56; Jeremiah 22; Ezekiel 18:1–9; Joel 2:13; Amos 5; Micah 4 and 6; Matthew 18, 22:34–40, 23:11–12, and 25:31–46; Luke 4:18–19 and 14; John 4; Acts 20:19; Romans 1:17; 2 Corinthians 6:6; Colossians 3:12; 1 Peter 5:5–6.
19. See Virginia Ramey Mollenkott, "Overcoming Heterosexism—To Benefit Everyone," in *Homosexuality in the Church*, ed. Jeffrey S. Siker (Louisville, Ky.: Westminster John Knox Press, 1994), 148. Of particular interest on same-sex marriages, as Mollenkott notes, "In other words, nine centuries before heterosexual marriage was declared a sacrament, the church liturgically celebrated same-sex covenants. The request of gay/lesbian people is that the contemporary church restore an ancient privilege."

Notes to Chapter 1: We Remember Our Baptism

1. *Book of Worship for Church and Home* (Nashville: The Methodist Publishing House, 1989), 390–91.
2. *Rauch* is the Hebrew word for breath, wind, and spirit. See Francis Brown et al., *The New Brown-Driver-Briggs Hebrew-English Lexicon of the Old Testament* (Peabody, Mass.: Hendrickson Publishers, 1979), 924. See also George V. Wigram, *The New Englishman's Hebrew Concordance* (Peabody, Mass.: Hendrickson Publishers, 1984), 1160.

3. Marilyn Alexander's reflection on *Freedom is Coming,* a South African freedom song.
4. *Book of Hymns* (Nashville: United Methodist Publishing House, 1966), No. 829.
5. Emily Yoffe, "The Double Life of Finis Crutchfield," in *Texas Monthly,* October 15, 1987, 102, 200.
6. Cf., *Texas Monthly,* 102, 195.
7. Cf., 193.
8. Ibid., 194–98.
9. See Penny Lernoux, *Cry of the People* (Garden City, N.J.: Doubleday, 1980); Phyllis Trible, *Texts of Terror* (Philadelphia: Fortress Press, 1984); Alice Walker, *The Color Purple* (New York: Washington Square Press, 1982).
10. See Letha D. Scanzoni and Virginia Ramey Mollenkott, *Is the Homosexual My Neighbor?* (San Francisco: Harper & Row, 1978). Revised and updated, HarperSanFrancisco, 1994.

Notes to Chapter 2: Silenced: Stories of Exclusion and Pain

1. Suzanne Pharr, *Homophobia* (Inverness, Calif.: Chardon Press, 1988).
2. Ibid., 1–2.
3. Joseph L. Allen, *Love and Conflict* (Nashville: Abingdon Press, 1984), 68.
4. Cf. James B. Nelson, *Body Theology* (Louisville, Ky.: Westminster/John Knox Press, 1992), 68.
5. *The 1992 United Methodist Book of Discipline* (Nashville: The United Methodist Publishing House, 1992), 92.
6. U.S. Department of Health and Human Services, "Report of the Secretary's Task Force on Youth Suicide," 1990, 3–110.
7. Craig O'Neill and Kathleen Ritter, *Coming Out Within* (San Francisco: HarperSanFrancisco, 1992), 5–7.
8. U.S. Department of Health and Human Services, "Report," 3–110.
9. Ibid., 127–28.
10. Pharr, *Homophobia,* 45.

Notes to Chapter 3: Strangers: Stories of Judgment

1. *American Heritage Dictionary of the English Language,* 3rd ed. (Boston: Houghton Mifflin Co., 1992), 1775.

2. Ibid., 629.
3. Francis Brown, et al., eds. *The New Brown-Driver-Briggs Hebrew-English Lexicon of the Old Testament* (Peabody, Mass.: Hendrickson Publishers, 1979), 158, 648.
4. Ibid., 158.
5. Bruce Hilton, *Can Homophobia Be Cured?* (Nashville: Abingdon Press, 1992), 68–69.
6. One of many references to hate-filled slogans and rhetoric of the religious right can be found in "Us vs. Them: On Battlefields from Portland, ME., to Portland, OR., the Religious Right's Crusade Against Gays and Lesbians Intensifies," *The Advocate* 2(641):41–45.
7. Marilyn Alexander, personal journal.
8. Carter Heyward, "Sexuality, Love and Justice," in *Weaving the Visions*, eds. Judith Plaskow and Carol Christ (San Francisco: HarperSanFrancisco, 1989), 297.
9. See Laurie Wilson, "Women Who Suffer Violence often Know Attacker," *Dallas Morning News*, January 31, 1994. Wilson states: "Two-thirds of the women who are victims of violent crimes are attacked by a husband, a boyfriend, a relative or acquaintance, a new Justice Department report says.

    "And women are 10 times more likely than men to be victimized by someone they know, the Bureau of Justice Statistics study found.

    "The report, released Monday, indicates that the American home is becoming an increasingly violent place for women, experts said.

    'It's always been a myth that it's safer for women in their own home,' said Rita Smith, coordinator for the National Coalition Against Domestic Violence in Denver. 'A large percentage of women would be safer on the street than at home. Most women believe that if someone loves you, they won't hurt you.'

    "Of the attacks on women, 28 percent of the offenders were intimates, such as husbands or boyfriends, and 39 percent were acquaintances or relatives, the report states."

    See Judith Lewis Herman, M.D., *Trauma and Recovery* (New York: Basic Books, 1992), 30. Herman states: "Sexual assaults against women and children were shown to be pervasive and endemic in our culture. The most sophisticated epidemiological survey was conducted in the early 1980s by Diana Russell, a sociologist and human rights activist. Over 900 women, chosen by random sampling techniques, were interviewed in depth about their experiences of domestic violence and sexual exploitation. The results were horrifying. One woman in four had been raped. One woman in three had been sexually abused in childhood."

See also Jan E. Stets and Murray A. Strauss, "The Marriage License as a Hitting License: A Comparison of Assaults in Dating, Cohabiting, and Married Couples," in *Violence in Dating Relationships: Emerging Social Issues,* eds. Maureen A. Pirog-Good and Jan E. Stets (New York: Praeger Publishers, 1989), 33. Stets and Strauss comment on the abuses in dating relationships, "The most recent research shows that dating violence is also pervasive and is a hidden serious social problem (Bogal-Allbritten & Allbritten, 1985). About 20 percent of college students have been physically assaulted by a dating partner (Makepeace, 1981; Cate et al., 1982; Stets & Pirog-Good, 1987)."

10. Suzanne Pharr, *Homophobia* (Inverness, Calif.: Chardon Press, 1988), 16–17.
11. Gary David Comstock, "Aliens in the Promised Land?" *Homosexuality and Religion* (New York: Haworth Press, 1990), 139–40.
12. Carter Heyward, *Touching Our Strength* (San Francisco: HarperSanFrancisco, 1989), 90.
13. Beverly Wilding Harrison, "Human Sexuality and Mutuality," in *Christian Feminism,* ed. Judith L. Wicdman (New York: Harper & Row, 1984), 153.
14. James B. Nelson, *Body Theology* (Louisville, Ky.: Westminster/John Knox Press, 1992), 37.
15. Ibid., 68–70.
16. David Crawford, *Easing the Ache* (New York: NAL-Dutton, 1991), 148.
17. Pharr, *Homophobia,* 1.
18. See Christine M. Smith, *Preaching as Weeping, Confession, and Resistance* (Louisville, Ky.: Westminster John/Knox Press, 1992), 2. Smith elaborates, "I have come to see the interlocking partners of oppression more clearly as handicappism, ageism, sexism, heterosexism, racism, and classism. . . . I now must name this interlocking mass of oppression 'radical evil.'"
19. Ibid., 88.

20. Pharr, *Homophobia*, 1, 2.
21. Bruce Hilton, *Can Homophobia Be Cured?* (Nashville: Abingdon Press, 1992), 72.
22. Pharr, *Homophobia*, 9.
23. Ibid.
24. Audre Lorde, *Sister Outsider*, (Trumansburg, N.Y.: Crossing Press, 1984), 49.
25. Ibid., 48.
26. Pharr, *Homophobia*, 19.
27. Mpho Tutu, Flathead Lake United Methodist Senior High Camp, Flathead Lake, Montana, August, 1992.

Notes to Chapter 4: Do This in Remembrance of Us

1. *United Methodist Hymnal* (Nashville: The United Methodist Publishing House, 1989), 40.
2. James F. White, *The Sacraments as God's Self-Giving* (Nashville: Abingdon Press, 1983), 34.
3. Cf. *United Methodist Hymnal*, 50–53.
4. White, *Sacraments*, 34.
5. Marjorie Procter-Smith, *In Her Own Rite* (Nashville: Abingdon Press, 1990), 146.
6. Schubert M. Ogden, Lecture, Perkins School of Theology, March 9, 1988.
7. White, *Sacraments*, 100.
8. Ibid., 101.
9. Ibid., 38.
10. Laurence Hull Stookey, *Baptism* (Nashville: Abingdon Press, 1982), 14.
11. White, *Sacraments*, 54.
12. Ibid., 52.
13. Ibid., 69.
14. Ibid., 94.
15. Ibid., 95–96.
16. Ibid., 99.

Notes to Chapter 5: And Be Thankful

1. It is important to note the change in attitude towards eunuchs and foreigners from earlier writings that excluded them (cf. Deut. 23). This passage in Isaiah gives us an example of how Is-

raelite thought and beliefs changed over time, not remaining static and unmoving as traditionally thought. The Church today can learn from the Israelite expanded thought. See also Kittredge Cherry and Zalmon Sherwood, eds. *Equal Rites* (Louisville, Ky.: Westminster John Knox Press, 1995), xviii.

2. Marjorie Procter-Smith, *In Her Own Rite*, (Nashville: Abingdon Press, 1990), 145.
3. Marilyn Alexander, personal journal.
4. Cf. Kay Longcope, "Death of a Texan," *The Advocate* 649:44–45. See also Frank Trejo, "Tyler Rally Offers Hope, Outrage," *Daily Morning News*, January 9, 1994, 37.
5. "Self-avowed practicing homosexual" is a term used to refer to gay and lesbian persons in *The 1992 United Methodist Book of Discipline* (Nashville: The United Methodist Publishing House, 1992), 92.
6. "Ten Simple Things You Can Do To Make a Difference," *Parents and Friends of Lesbians and Gays*, 1993.
7. Galatians 3:28.
8. See also Psalm 148 and Job 39—41. See Carol A. Newsom, "Job," in *The Women's Bible Commentary*, eds. Carol A. Newsom and Sharon H. Ringe (Louisville, Ky.: Westminster/John Knox Press, 1992), 136. Newsom notes that in Job, God is trying to reorient Job to an image of God, one that delights in the wildness of creation. "What God has done by ignoring Job's way of posing the question is to illumine the inadequacy of Job's starting point, his legal model of rights and faults and his image of God as the great patriarch. . . . This new image is one of God as a power for life, balancing the needs of all creatures, not just humans, cherishing freedom, full of fierce love and delight for each thing without regard for its utility, acknowledging the deep interconnectedness of death and life, restraining and nurturing each element in the ecology of all creation. It is a description of God and the world that has strong points of contact with contemporary feminist thought."
9. Irene Monroe, "The Aché Sisters," in *Women at Worship*, eds. Marjorie Procter-Smith and Janet R. Walton (Louisville, Ky.: Westminster/John Knox Press, 1993), 128.
10. Ibid., 130.
11. Robert Goss, *Jesus Acted Up* (San Francisco: HarperSanFrancisco, 1994), 123–24. Goss notes, "A Christian change or base community is a local community of resistance made up of dis-

enfranchised exiles or oppressed people who are committed to actively and politically changing oppressive structures."

12. The term "act-up" has taken on new meaning since the inception and important work of ACTUP (AIDS Coalition to Unleash Power) which is a "non-partisan group of diverse individuals united in anger and committed to direct action to end the AIDS crisis" (Goss, *Jesus Acted Up*, 151). Taken out of the context of fighting the deadly destructive disease of AIDS and the powers and systems that prevent active fight for a cure, this group is often shrugged off as militant troublemakers out to promote the "gay agenda." In the context of a pandemic, it is a sign of righteous and just upheaval, matched to the destructive forces of the disease and the immediate need for action. Jesus also acted upon urgent desire for healing and justice for all people—for the reign of God.

13. Goss, *Jesus Acted Up*, 37.

14. Ibid., 38.

15. Ibid., 129.

16. Marilyn Alexander, personal journal.

17. In many mainline churches, gay/lesbian and straight Christians have joined together to call their own denominations and their own congregations to remember gay and lesbian Christians and be thankful. Ecumenically, the movement is known as the "welcoming movement" and consists of congregations and campus ministries that publicly declare that they are welcoming gay/lesbian/bisexual persons as full participants in the life and the work of that community of faith. "The welcoming programs highlight the particular situation of gay, lesbian, and bisexual persons today because of the blatant discrimination they currently experience in our church and society" (*OPEN HANDS*, 863), 10. The "welcoming movement" is a hopeful glimpse of the body of Christ finally ending the silence and acknowledging that gay/lesbian Christians are not strangers. They are very much a part of the family. "Welcoming" churches and campus ministries prophetically witness to their denominations about God's call for grace and justice, and they act as sacramental parts of a journey in which they call the Church to remember and be thankful. See Chris Glaser, "The Love that Dare Not Pray its Name: The Gay and Lesbian Movement in America's Churches," in *Homosexuality in the Church*, ed. Jeffrey S. Siker (Louisville, Ky.: Westminster John Knox Press, 1994).

18. Carter Heyward, *Touching Our Strength* (San Francisco: HarperSanFrancisco, 1989), 21.
19. Virginia Ramey Mollenkott, "Overcoming Heterosexism—To Benefit Everyone," in *Homosexuality in the Church*, ed. Jeffrey S. Siker (Louisville, Ky.: Westminster John Knox Press, 1994), 147.
20. John 15:15.
21. Judith Lewis Herman, M.D., *Trauma and Recovery* (New York: Basic Books, 1992), 197.
22. Marilyn Alexander, personal journal.
23. Carter Heyward, *Touching our Strength*, 104–5.
24. Congregations can explore new possibilities for creative and inclusive liturgy which affirms the full participation of gay/lesbians in the church. A helpful worship resource is Kittredge Cherry and Zalmon Sherwood, eds. *Equal Rites* (Louisville, Ky.: Westminster John Knox Press, 1995).
25. Janie Spahr was called to be associate pastor for the Downtown United Presbyterian Church in Rochester, New York, as an open lesbian. Her call was later challenged and blocked by the National Church Court. She now serves as National Evangelist Educator in order to help people understand the need for acceptance of gay/lesbian/bisexual persons and their right to serve the church. Spahr spoke with Alexander during a break at the Re-Imagining Conference, November 1993, Minneapolis, Minnesota.
26. Carter Heyward, *Touching our Strength*, 35.
27. Ibid., 70.
28. Suzanne Pharr, *Homophobia* (Inverness, Calif.: Chardon Press, 1988), 52.
29. German theologian and pastor Martin Niemoller's quote about Hitler's Nazi party (1933–1945) and its genocidal policies appears in *Congressional Record*, October 14, 1968, 316–36. "When Hitler attacked the Jews I was not a Jew, therefore, I was not concerned. And when Hitler attacked the Catholics, I was not a Catholic, and therefore, I was not concerned. And when Hitler attacked the unions and the industrialists, I was not a member of the unions and I was not concerned. Then, Hitler attacked me and the Protestant church—and there was nobody left to be concerned."
30. Pharr, *Homophobia*, 53.
31. Ibid., 64.

◆ Bibliography

Allen, Joseph L. *Love and Conflict: A Covenantal Model of Christian Ethics.* Nashville: Abingdon Press, 1984.

American Heritage Dictionary of the English Language, 3d ed. Boston: Houghton Mifflin Co., 1992.

Biddle, Lindsey Louise. "Hospitable Interpretations of Sodom and Gomorrah." *OPEN HANDS* 9:18–20.

Book of Hymns. Nashville: The Methodist Publishing House, 1966.

Book of Worship for Church and Home. Nashville: The Methodist Publishing House, 1989.

Brown, Francis, et al., eds. *The New Brown-Driver-Briggs Hebrew-English Lexicon of the Old Testament.* Peabody, Mass.: Hendrickson Publishers, 1979.

Cherry, Kittredge and Zalmon Sherwood, eds. *Equal Rites: Lesbian and Gay Worship, Ceremonies, and Celebrations.* Louisville, Ky.: Westminster John Knox Press, 1995.

Comstock, Gary David. "Aliens in the Promised Land?: Keynote Address for the 1986 National Gathering of the United Church of Christ's Coalition for Lesbian/Gay Concerns," in *Homosexuality and Religion,* pref. Richard Hasbany. New York: Haworth Press, 1990.

Crawford, David. *Easing the Ache: Gay Men Recovering from Compulsive Behaviors.* New York: NAL-Dutton, 1991.

Edwards, George R. *Gay-Lesbian Liberation: A Biblical Perspective.* New York: Pilgrim Press, 1984.

Fewell, Danna Nolan and David M. Gunn. *Gender, Power and Promise: Stories of Desire & Division in the Hebrew Bible.* Nashville: Abingdon Press, 1993.

Furnish, Victor Paul. *Moral Teachings of Paul: Selected Issues*. Nashville: Abingdon Press, 1985.

———— "Some Perspectives on the Bible and Homosexuality," in *Christian Argument for Gays and Lesbians in the Military: Essays by Mainline Church Leaders*. Introduction by John J. Carey. Lewiston, N.Y.: Edwin Mellen Press, 1993.

Gomes, Peter J. "Homophobic? Re-Read Your Bible." *New York Times*, August 17, 1992.

Goss, Robert. *Jesus Acted Up: A Gay and Lesbian Manifesto*. San Francisco: HarperSanFrancisco, 1994.

Gottwald, Norman K. *The Hebrew Bible—A Socio-Literary Introduction*. Philadelphia: Fortress Press, 1985.

Harrison, Beverly Wilding. "Human Sexuality and Mutuality," in *Christian Feminism: Visions of a New Humanity*. Edited by Judith L. Weidman. New York: Harper & Row, 1984.

Herman, Judith Lewis, M.D., *Trauma and Recovery: The Aftermath of Violence—From Domestic Abuse to Political Terror*. New York: Basic Books, 1992.

Heyward, Carter. "Sexuality, Love and Justice," in *Weaving the Visions: New Patterns in Feminist Spirituality*. Edited by Judith Plaskow and Carol Christ. San Francisco: HarperSanFrancisco, 1989.

Heyward, Carter. *Touching Our Strength: The Erotic as Power and the Love of God*. San Francisco: HarperSanFrancisco, 1989.

Hilton, Bruce. *Can Homophobia Be Cured? Wrestling with Questions That Challenge the Church*. Nashville: Abingdon Press, 1992.

Horner, Tom. *Jonathan Loved David: Homosexuality in Biblical Times*. Philadelphia: Westminster Press, 1978.

Lorde, Audre. *Sister Outsider: Essays and Speeches*. Trumansburg, N.Y.: Crossing Press, 1984.

McClain, George D. "What Does the Bible Say about Homosexuality?" *Social Questions Bulletin* 83:2–3.

Milgrom, Jacob. "Does the Bible Prohibit Homosexuality?" *Bible Review*, December, 1993.

Mollenkott, Virginia Ramey. "Overcoming Heterosexism—To Benefit Everyone," in *Homosexuality in the Church: Both Sides of the Debate*. Edited by Jeffrey S. Siker. Louisville, Ky.: Westminster John Knox Press, 1994.

Monroe, Irene. "The Aché Sisters: Discovering the Power of the Erotic in Ritual," in *Women at Worship: Interpretations of North American Diversity*. Edited by Marjorie Procter-Smith and Janet R. Walton. Louisville, Ky.: Westminster/John Knox Press, 1993.

Nelson, James B. *Body Theology*. Louisville, Ky.: Westminster/John Knox Press, 1992.

Newsom, Carol A. "Job," in *The Women's Bible Commentary*. Edited by Carol A. Newsom and Sharon H. Ringe. Louisville, Ky.: Westminster/John Knox Press, 1992.

O'Neill, Craig and Kathleen Ritter. *Coming Out Within: Stages of Spiritual Awakening for Lesbians and Gay Men*. San Francisco: HarperSanFrancisco, 1992.

Pharr, Suzanne. *Homophobia: A Weapon of Sexism*. Inverness, Calif.: Chardon Press, 1988.

Procter-Smith, Marjorie. *In Her Own Rite: Constructing Feminist Liturgical Tradition*. Nashville: Abingdon Press, 1990.

"Report of the Secretary's Task Force on Youth Suicide," U.S. Department of Health and Human Services, Washington, D.C., 1990.

Siker, Jeffrey S., ed. *Homosexuality in the Church: Both Sides of the Debate*. Louisville, Ky.: Westminster John Knox Press, 1994.

Smith, Christine M. *Preaching as Weeping, Confession, and Resistance: Radical Responses to Radical Evil*. Louisville, Ky.: Westminster/John Knox Press, 1992.

Spong, John Shelby. *Rescuing the Bible from Fundamentalism: A Bishop Rethinks the Meaning of Scripture*. San Francisco: HarperSanFrancisco, 1992.

Stookey, Laurence Hull. *Baptism: Christ's Act in the Church*. Nashville: Abingdon Press, 1982.

1992 United Methodist The Book of Discipline. Nashville: The United Methodist Publishing House, 1992.

United Methodist Hymnal. Nashville: The United Methodist Publishing House, 1989.

White, James F. *The Sacraments as God's Self-Giving*. Nashville: Abingdon Press, 1983.

Wigram, George. V. *The New Englishman's Hebrew Concordance*. Peabody, Mass.: Hendrickson Publishers, 1984.

Yoffe, Emily. "The Double Life of Finis Crutchfield." *Texas Monthly*, October 15, 1987.